The Awkward Phase

The Uplifting Tales of Those Weird Kids You Went to

High School With

Tyler Gillespie and Claire Linic

D1370649

Skyhorse Publishing

*Dedicated to our families, both given and chosen.
We're looking at you, Lynnae.*

Visit our website at www.skyhorsepublishing.com.

10 9 8 7 6 5 4 3 2 1

Library of Congress Cataloging-in-Publication Data is available on file.

Cover design by Brian Peterson
Cover photos provided by contributors

Print ISBN: 978-1-63220-349-6
Ebook ISBN: 978-1-63220-802-6

Printed in China

Contents

"To the world you might just be one person but to one person you might be their world."

Tyler made this awkward-embracing (great) piece of art back during his senior year of high school (2005). Yes, we think it's awesome, too.

The Awkward Phase

O h, hi there. We're so glad to see you're picking up our book, and that your hair is looking great right now. Not to be forward (though foreword), but this is when we're supposed to introduce ourselves, so nice to meet you and here goes.

In the moments between YouTube video dance parties in our work break room,* we decided to create some type of comedy project that wasn't biting or sarcastic—two realities we had sometimes experienced during our other comedic pursuits.

Everyone had an awkward phase, we thought. *Those times made us who we are today.*

Nearly a year and a half before *The Awkward Phase* thought, we had met on our first day of a part-time job at a museum in Chicago's Hyde Park, where, fun fact, President Obama owns a house (we've never been, please invite us for dinner, and we'll bring a dish). As the story is remembered, on that day in October we were two of the earliest birds, still not used to public transit. We sat next to each other at a

---

* To any of our future employers, we'd like to note we were on unpaid breaks. We're really hard workers. HIRE US.

small round table, near escalators leading up to the place that made *a choice* to hire us. As we filled out paperwork, we chatted about our home states Florida and Nebraska. Neither of us had lived in Chicago for long, and finding a partner in the struggle of oft-maligned states, we immediately bonded. Sunshine-state stereotypes and corn jokes. Awkward kid recognizes awkward kid.

For a few months after this first day, we went our separate work-ways—off to different departments. Our paths often crossed, but we were both so busy stress-crying and dealing with the impending winter that we didn't have much time for anything besides *it's really cold, bye*. As luck—also known as a horizontal departmental transition—would have it, in the summer we ended up on the same work team, in a huge movie theater. We dubbed it "the darkest and coldest place in the city."

The Awkward Phase started in our break room, away from the field-trip kids talking about love and life during the movie we were supposed to monitor. The break room was a small space with carpeted walls and no windows. It looked more like a padded room than a place for midday coffee binges. But, maybe it's a metaphor—or, more likely, maybe it's not.

Anyway, we needed a laugh.

After we threw around some ideas—like mom-style[†]—we settled on what we had most in common and what people don't usually like to talk about: our awkwardness.

[†] We're still kind of into this idea. Moms are awesome.

Start Flashback *Back in the '90s, when slap bracelets and Velcro ruled supreme, two adolescents stumbled around on gangly limbs. One, Claire Linic, had permed her bowl cut, and the other, Tyler Gillespie, had recently purchased self-tanner and told the cashier it was for his girlfriend. Those moments were first-day-of-school rough. But, looking back, we thought those days were actually kind of awesome, because DAY-GLO and BOWL CUTS.* **End Flashback**

From our Florida-Nebraska talk on the first workday, our awkwardness acted as a summer-camp friendship bracelet. With our combined decades of awkward life, this idea was such a perfect fit it wasn't even funny. No . . . wait, it was funny—we're trying to get you to buy this book. It's super funny! We survived our awkward teenage years, and as almost-thriving twenty-somethings, we decided to ask ourselves a question. *If we could talk to our fourteen-year-old selves, what would we tell them?*

Looking back at our stories and pictures, we realized how often our brace-face years stay hidden in the cynical shadows. At first we were embarrassed of the people in those photos; they had acne and people made fun of their big ears. We thought bringing these pictures—the people we were—to light would further open us to schoolyard name-calling. But, in an Oprah-esque moment of clarity, we realized these stories need to be told, because part of being okay with who you are now is respecting each stage of your life. The kids in those pictures have been teased enough. We'll give you a quick break here to grab a pen and jot down a note to your former self. Seriously, you'll probably be glad you did.

We launched *The Awkward Phase* with the aim of inspiring people to celebrate their awkward years rather than disown them. Our goal is for people to feel more comfortable with the past, which, for a lot of people, was filled with loads of insecurity. In sharing these stories, we also believe it helps youngsters who currently feel weighed down by their awkwardness. *The Awkward Phase* reclaims those years when you might not have felt cool, but that helped turn you into the awesome and empathetic adult you are today. Everyone has had an awkward phase—even Jennifer Aniston has said she did!—so let's learn to love those pictures we once wanted to burn.

In the following pages, we have collected triumphantly awkward stories from seasoned comedians to YouTube stars to our family members. In these pages, you will read about a boy who realized he was gay because of Richard Simmons, a girl who obsessively wrote to Reba McEntire, and Rat-Boy. There are Mall Glamour Shots, Picnic Costumes, and *Teenage Mutant Ninja Turtles*. We've got Beanie Babies, American Girl Dolls, and Fearless Rascals. Oh, and a mother's advice on school picture day.

Feel free to laugh—it's what helped our contributors learn to love these times of their lives. Unlike other books that take a more biting schoolyard stance, with *The Awkward Phase*, everyone is in on the joke. You don't have to eat your lunch alone in the bathroom stall. You can sit with us. This is a book about owning your awkward. This is a story of *your* triumph.

XOXO,

Tyler Gillespie and Claire Linic

Note to Readers

People all over the country graciously sent us their photos and stories. We've tried to keep these accounts as true to their own voices as possible. Edits were made for clarity, length, and speling [sic]. Most contributors changed the names of other people in their submission(s) to protect the innocent. If you know a person, and you think there's a resemblance to you, we'd suggest taking it as a compliment—you made an impression. These pages are filled with awesome, and we couldn't have done it without each and every one of the awkward kids.

Tyler as a Pilgrim, because, 'tis the season and all.

Chapter 1

Excuses to Dress Up

I'M THE PICNIC TABLE NEXT TO SEXY CATS
Claire Linic

This picture tells a story—a very loud and obvious story. To everyone, it seems, except thirteen-year-old me.

I've had my fair share of awkward phases, and then went back for seconds. But usually I've been aware of them. Like as I write this I have a rattail, and I acknowledge that (growing out a pixie is not for the faint of heart). However, you could have never told that ecstatic teen dressed as a picnic table something was off here. I had spent the whole day making the costume and just knew in my heart everyone loved it as much as me.

Couldn't I see my friends were too cool for me? Why hadn't I worked on my sexy hip-popped pose? I was too busy giving a thumbs-up and middle-part salute to the costume I made. I see you, thirteen-year-old Claire, and I respect you. Don't worry, baby, we made it out of 2002 okay.

We are still awkward, our friends are still cooler than us, but we are happy.

MY ARBY'S SWIMSUIT PHOTOS
Kelly Bird

As a young female, even at age ten, I was already aware that my teeny-tiny adorable blond sister had hit the gene pool jackpot, and I was already despising my training bra and worrying about my weight. She noshed on pizza rolls, while I substituted my fries for a side salad. It's hard being a girl.

It was 1995, and I loved working on my bug collection, reading *Goosebumps*, and playing Barbies (but only in secret).

Each summer our parents took us to get photos taken at the only "professional" photographer in our small town, Peter Bahr—pronounced *Petah Bah* because of his thick German accent. The only thing more potent than his BO was the lime green color of his house where his studio was located . . . in the hot attic.

My parents generally blew these photos up to just under poster size and hung them all over the house, so we had to be prepared with multiple wardrobe changes, curling irons on standby, and hairspray at the ready. The best photos by Petah Bah were displayed for an entire month in the Arby's on Third Street, and we made the cut every single year. Because there were five restaurants in town, every person we had ever known in our entire lives was bound to grab a roast beef there within a month's time and check out the "artwork."

This year, as my sister and I finished up our first round of photos, I found out swimsuits were up next. Yuck! Mine was a blast to swim in at the pool, but posing in it under a hot spotlight was the ultimate embarrassment for me. I was so nervous for these photos and what I might look like in them.

I never stood a chance in my quest to skip the swimsuit photos. My mom thought it was precious, my dad was trying to keep my mom happy, and my sister was just trying to get out of there so she could go home and climb a tree. I figured if I pouted hard enough, we might just leave because even my mom wouldn't find *those* pictures precious, right?!

CLICK *SNAP*

The horror and unhappiness directed at my swimsuit is written all over my face. I wore my heart on my sleeve. I still wear it there to this day. Even at ten, I knew I was being ridiculous and I sucked it up.

I'll admit some of those photos are just the littlest bit precious.

WE ARE STILL THESE WEIRD LITTLE GIRLS

Jane Hammer

My sister is going to kill me. She'll probably be super embarrassed about this picture, but I'm going to spend my time trying to convince her why she—and I—shouldn't be.

Look at us.

Yes, we're covered in plastic bags. We were bored and decided to make costumes out of the old grocery store bags our parents kept under the sink. Do you remember how much fun that was?

I do.

I remember running around the yard, creating characters and lives and backstories for these weird bag people who came out of thin air to us. We were creative, and we never backed away from it. This was a time before insecurity set in. This was a time before we started fighting over me stealing your clothes or wanting to hang out with you and your cool friends. This was a time before the Internet.

When it was just the two of us, we were truly ourselves in a way that is hard to ever recreate. We had to be creative when we'd exhausted all of our old games. We had to come up with games ourselves.

We have gone through a lot in the years since this photo. I don't remember how old we were, but I know that we didn't know enough to be embarrassed. There are many days when I long for that brazen confidence. That was before we knew any better.

Do you remember how weird our parents let us be?

We were lucky to be encouraged to make costumes and prance around our yard in our own little world. We should be proud of these strange little girls, never embarrassed.

Let's promise to avoid insecurity as much as we can. Let's try and value these little girls as much as we can. They didn't care what anyone thought. Without these little girls, we'd never be the people we are today.

And, just to clarify, we are still just as weird but there are fewer costumes involved.

TREK LIFE
Mitchell Lyon

I still consider this outfit pretty cool. But maybe the fact that I owned the official *Star Trek: The Next Generation* tricorder and communication badge doesn't help my case. I was enormously proud and took every opportunity to recite the entire *Next Generation* crew and rank, along with the corresponding actors' names. I also collected the entire *Next Generation* figurine series along with replica engineering and bridge play sets. I know what you're thinking, and yes, they connected with working automatic doors, blinking lights, and real *Star Trek* sound effects.

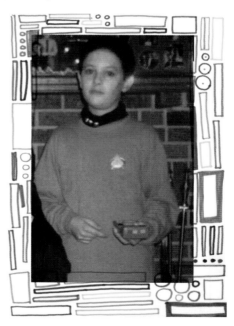

People can say what they will, but I'm sure Brent Spiner would be quite proud of this eleven-year-old's version of the beloved android named Data.

HOBO DEBBIE GIBSON: A BRIEF HALLOWEEN RETROSPECTIVE

Caroline Harrington

Halloween 1986

Even at a young age, I remember my first Halloween in Wallingford, Connecticut, as being really visceral.

It was 1986. My family had just moved to Connecticut from California. I was very impressed with Halloween in New England, as it was the it-event of fall even more so than Thanksgiving because by November, the weather was gross and people went into hibernation mode.

Our two best friends were Derek and Tommy, who shared our ages and lived down the street. Our costumes were a little more slapped together than usual, as my frazzled parents were surely still in the

midst of unpacking. I wanted to go as a witch and wouldn't go out trick-or-treating without the only broom in the house. Here is smug six-year-old me with my damn broom, clearly thinking that I looked like the coolest witch on the block. Twenty-eight years later, all I can think when I see this picture is: "Weiner!"

Halloween 1988

"Hobo Debbie Gibson."

Yes, this was the name of my costume. No further explanation needed.

Halloween 1989

I wore this sweater at least three times a week for a year or more. I loved it so much, I built my Halloween costume around it. I wanted red pants and my mom wouldn't go out and buy me a new pair. Instead, I wore red tights (before I knew that leggings/tights were not pants). They were very opaque, but still.

My best friend Sarah (also pictured in 1988) went as a rich lady. She wore one of my mother's old ice skating dresses, and the whole night, I was secretly jealous.

Our costumes were always very slapdash but not because we didn't care. We were more excited about being out in the night on our own (our neighborhood was really safe, and we knew everyone) and plotting our course. We went out mostly with pillowcases instead of bags and would draw a map of the neighborhood weeks before, adding stars to the houses that had given out the best candy the year before.

I'm pretty sure this was the starting point for my love of infographics.

HELLO. MY NAME'S FORREST. FORREST GUMP

Jessica Stopak

For third grade "Idol Day," I spend two whole days putting together the best costume. Mom and I sit in front of the TV rewinding the VHS (yep . . .VHS) of *Forrest Gump* and watching the moment when the briefcase opens just so we can get every detail exactly right.

In third grade, Tom could do no wrong. *Forrest Gump* was played over and over on my TV. The ensemble was part goodwill, part house-found items, and all heart. I pulled all my hair back to appear to be a man. The hat read, "Bubba Gump Shrimp Co." Before it was a restaurant. Very serious. The briefcase was filled with the exact items found in the movie. When the judges came to the room, I offered each of them a chocolate, saying, "Life's like a box of chocolates, you never know what you're gonna get," in my best Southern Forrest twang.

All my VHS-watching is worth it when I am awarded first place throughout the whole school for my re-creation of my idol.

People comment on how odd/funny/unfortunate/amazing it is that I chose to go as a man. All I was thinking was I love this actor. Why would I go as anyone else? The next year I went as my next favorite actor: Jim Carrey as Ace Ventura, Pet Detective. Stuffed monkey and all.

I won't end this story until we talk about my surroundings. Yes. Those are stenciled flowers as my border. Yes. Those are *Beauty and the Beast* stickers that my mother painstakingly applied to my wall one afternoon. Yes. That is a hideous old-fashioned heating blanket. And I know that every little girl had a ruffle curtain in her room in the '90s.

As funny as this picture looks now . . . I was just an average girl with male actors for idols. Tom Hanks is an amazing actor. *Forrest Gump* is an inspiring movie. *Beauty and the Beast* is a "Tale as old as time."

This picture hangs proudly on my wall in my twenty-six-year-old room. What a great day.

PS: A big thanks to my mother, who worked with me to quickly put together this amazing costume! She is a constant supporter of my passions to this day. She's an amazing woman!

BUG BITES
Taylor Wolfe

I was invited to my first coed party in the eighth grade, and it was a big deal. Folded triangle notes were circulating the junior high all week in preparation. It was a Halloween party so most of the girls decided to dress up as bugs.

But unfortunately for me, I had done something to piss off the queen bee that week and wasn't invited to her house for the pre-party, the house where all of the girls were getting ready together.

I said *screw it* and decided to just show up with the best bug costume I could find and show them all. My mom helped me paint my face, and while you can't see my blue Nikes in the photo, I assure you they are wrapped in black tape. It was all going so well until I actually got to the party and realized in absolute horror that the other girls all chose to dress as "slutty bugs." They were wearing those short Soffee shorts with tight white shirts they had puff-painted on with names like "sexy spider" and "baby butterfly." They didn't look anything like bugs.

Everything I had on was completely wrong, including the (very unnecessary) fleece red-and-black gloves I was initially so excited about. But it gets worse. One of the mean boys, let's call him Andy, because that was his name, could smell my insecurity and he suddenly announced in front of everyone, "It's okay, Taylor's wearing so many layers to hide her bug bites."

To which I snapped back, "It's October, I don't have any bug bites, dork!"

It seemed like a logical response to me. But I would later learn Andy was actually referring to my flat, ten-year-old boy-like chest. The slutty bugs had all developed. This ladybug had not.

Nearly twelve years later I wish I could tell all the flat-chested teenage girls out there to wear their bug bites proud!

While I never grew the chest I thought I would, at least I've never had a back problem either.

MY TIME TO SHINE . . . AT LEAST, THAT'S WHAT I THOUGHT

Helene Sula

In eighth grade I had the confidence most twenty-one-year-olds have on their birthday after five buttery nipple shots. My self-assurance came despite my dishwater-dull blond hair, height of a fifth grader, and slightly crooked teeth (I'd later wear braces, getting them off the November of senior year). My confidence mainly came from my theater teachers, who praised my undying love for singing show tunes and acting timid as the lead role in *Cinderella*.

Fridays at my Catholic school meant All-School Mass. I looked forward to this hour away from class, and I would situate myself near my best friend. We usually sat behind the pimply faced boy I had a crush on, so I could daydream about him as we spoke-sang the "Our Father." Toward the end of eighth grade, all theater kids were forced to audition for the end-of-the-year performance at the church. We would be congratulating our priest for winning the NCEA award—a big to-do, but as for actually what the award was for, I'll never know. But I knew the entire school, parents, and even the bishop were invited to attend. It would be my time to shine.

I, of course, auditioned. Along with seven other eighth graders, I made the cut. I rehearsed after school for weeks before the performance. I practiced my kicks in the mirror at home. The day of the performance I wasn't nervous—just ready to win the hearts of all those around me.

Maybe I can get a gig out of this, skip high school, and move right on to the Disney Channel or Nickelodeon. I'll pick up a steady drinking habit along the way if necessary.

As the piano teacher struck the first note of the show, the audience hushed. We walked down the aisle of the church. Top hats cocked, we began to sing the letters "NCEA" to the tune of "YMCA." Classic. I looked out into the audience with a surge of adrenaline. The kick-line started, but I was in my own world. Front and center. I continued on with the song, though this was the musical break. The piano teacher was so thrown off by my singing that she stopped playing and the crumpled noise of the piano ceased as wide eyes gazed at me. Then, I noticed—I was still singing.

After a beat, I stepped forward, removed my black top hat, and took a bow. I scooted back in the kick-line and nodded at the piano teacher to begin again.

When the performance ended, I hid from the crowd in the choir room behind the altar. The priest and award winner found me and seeing my red, tear-streaked face said, "Well, you got what you wanted." I looked up, puzzled and dismayed.

"Honey, you stole the show."

I wiped my tears, put back on the top hat, and walked out with my head held high.

I haven't stopped singing or kick-lining ever since. And now, every time I make a scene, I remember, at least I'm the star of the show.

My Obsession

Smile as bright as sunshine
Teeth like sparkling pearls
Watching that magical smile move through the hall
Blinded by beauty
Being led into a dark enchanged forest
Never able to escape the grasp of his eyes
They won't let me go
Entangled in an invisible net
  My Obsession

Yours

My heart beats for you
My mind thinks for you
I own nothing it's all yours
I see nothing you own my sight
You hear then let me listen
Who am I, not myself
You hold my emotions on your shelf.

Teen poems by Meagan Johnson

Chapter 2

BFFs, Crushes, and Other Secrets

HOCUS POCUS
Gaby Dunn

Though I met Jessilyn in Hebrew school, our friendship was entirely based on a mutual interest in the occult.

We were seven and, I guess, both bored with our "normal" suburban lives and had seen the same movie, maybe *Hocus Pocus* or *Buffy*. We were obsessed with the idea that we had secret powers and that we were more than just the average little girls everyone saw. Call it the Harry Potter Effect. We were waiting for our Hogwarts letters in a big way. Every time we hung out at her house, we'd lock ourselves in her bedroom and steal spoons from her mother's kitchen. Then, we'd "bend" them with our eyes, staring into the long mirror on her door, trying to "jump" into an alternate universe, and squinting at stuffed animals in the hopes we'd set them on fire with our mind.

We'd record our witchy progress in her journal and swear up and down that the other girl had definitely moved the spoon at least a little bit this time. We were obsessed with being powerful. We were kids, so every aspect of our lives was controlled. But in play, we were secretly in charge.

One afternoon, my mom took me to the public library to check out new books. I sneaked into the Occult section and somehow managed to take home a huge, dusty tome of ancient spells. I don't remember how I got it past my mom or if it was really an old book of magic or some New Age Wiccan "spell book for the modern womyn."

I brought the book home and hid it in my bathroom, where it stayed for a few years, unopened. Until puberty hit.

Though they say young girls are generally more sexually advanced than boys, crushes started kind of early for me. From third grade until eighth, I was "in love with" a boy in my year. The feelings I had for this boy could only be categorized as "desperate." He was popular—part of a group of four of the most athletic boys in our grade who by middle school started calling themselves the Final Four. He was half-Mexican and half-Spanish with a pale face full of adorable freckles, dark hair, and a body built from playing soccer. He was a cool kid.

I, on the other hand, was a hopeless nerd. (Are we shocked by this? I hid a spell book in my bathroom. Did you think I was going to turn out to be popular? *Pay attention*.) I wanted to be a famous writer. I read a lot. I wrote all the time in my flurry of notebooks and was constantly walking into walls because my head was in a novel. Not that this boy wasn't smart, too—he was.

In fact, the only motivation for us to talk to each other came after IQ test scores were revealed in the beginning of middle school.

"Looks like we're the two smartest kids in our grade," he said to me in the lunch line. I simply nodded, my illustrious vocabulary dribbling out the sides of my ears. In sixth grade, I finally broke out the spell book. I flipped to the page for love spells. I wish I remembered the exact spell, but I don't. I think it definitely involved me having to steal from him—I think the spell required something he'd touched, because I remember going into his locker during lunch and ripping pages from a math notebook inside. Either way, I was insane in the way only a middle school girl could be.

In my bathroom at home, I put all the ingredients into a wooden bowl from my family's kitchen and set them on fire with matches from the junk drawer. I chanted the spell.

"Is something burning?" my dad asked, banging on the bathroom door.

"No!" I shouted, coughing. "Just lighting a candle!"

I cleaned up as best I could, but there were ashes stuck in the crevices of the bathroom tile a year later when, still pining away silently for this boy who barely spoke to me, I began IMing him, asking arbitrary questions for homework assignments. The spell hadn't exactly worked, but he was at least writing back to my chats. I considered it a victory.

I was so obsessed with him that at the end of every—inevitably five- to ten-line—"conversation," I would print out the transcript and keep it in a navy blue binder hidden in the back of my closet. When I was feeling depressed, I would reread my favorite parts or highlight lines I felt were important to share with my one trust-worthy friend at school, a girl named Alex.

Alex was new, having transferred from public school. She wore gold jewelry and her bangs gelled down to her forehead. She was really into the Olsen twins and making mix CDs. She was petite and sometimes showed me links to pro-anorexia websites, which wor-ried me. She also had a crush on this same boy, but instead of it driv-ing us apart, our mutual love made us best friends.

I enjoyed hanging out with Alex and talking endlessly about this boy more than I ever really cared about dating him. Alex and I would spend weekends sleeping over at each other's houses and coming up with new nicknames for him or theories about whom he liked. We shared everything, as two best girlfriends can.

Then, tragedy struck. For high school, the object of our affection transferred to a public school. We lost touch with each other, inasmuch as we were ever "in touch" with each other. Alex also moved schools after eighth grade, and we stopped talking every day. I thought both relationships were simultaneously over.

Until the end of my senior year.

I'd spent most of ninth grade cleaning up my act. My skin cleared. I bought a hair straightener. I stopped caring what people thought. By the time I was a senior, I was still a virgin, but I considered myself open-minded and sexually liberated. I'd had a boyfriend for a year whom I'd been reluctant to sleep with because, ironically, I thought he was too obsessed with me. We'd just broken up. And then, in April, *he* resurfaced. My crush.

I'd gone to a house party with a female friend at an apartment complex. Turned out the apartment actually belonged to another original member of the Final Four I hadn't seen in years but with whom said friend was still friends.

I walked inside, and as the bong smoke parted, there he was. He didn't look that different. He'd maintained a "baby face," and though he was no longer what I'd consider my "type," and though I hadn't thought of him in years, I felt a strong urge to show him how much I'd changed. I needed to prove I wasn't the pathetic girl on the other end of those AIM conversations.

He remembered me, and we chatted about the last four years, standing in the kitchen, red Solo cups in hand. When he left the party that night, he asked for my number and programmed it into his phone. I literally did a jig to my parked car. He was attracted to me. I had won. But it wasn't enough.

A couple weeks later, after we'd been talking on the phone for a while, I asked if he'd be interested in coming to my prom. All his old friends from middle school would be there (I hadn't changed schools), and he'd get to party with them one last time before college if he came as my date. He accepted.

I don't remember anything about the actual prom other than that it took place on a boat and I wore a vintage 1950s dress with elbow-length silk black gloves, which no one appreciated.

After, everyone convened to get drunk at a nearby hotel.

I did shots and then, full of liquid courage, practically dragged my date into a vacant room. We made out in our underpants and dry humped until he came.

Then, I said the most charming and brave thing I ever have: "You know, next time, we could, uh, do it . . . for real."

He was flabbergasted. "Really?" he choked out.

"Sure," I said, trying to seem casual. "Next time we hang out, bring condoms."

The next time we hung out was two days later. He invited me to a hotel on the beach where his friends were throwing a summer pre-college party. After a few minutes of making nice with every-one, we excused ourselves and went into the bedroom. And then he revealed the best part: he was a virgin, too. We had sex. It was fine and normal. But inside, I was dying. Not only had I successfully lost my virginity to the boy I'd been silently in love with for most of my adolescence, I had also punched his V-card. If it hadn't seemed in bad form, I would have high-fived myself during the act.

We cuddled and he kept asking if I was truly okay, which I really, really was.

I don't want to say the spell I cast when I was twelve years old had worked, because I wasn't really in love with this boy anymore, and he hadn't majestically fallen in love with me. If anything, our consummation had broken a different spell. One in which my childhood rejections had convinced me I wasn't "cool" or worthy of the things I wanted. I could head off to college knowing I wasn't the nerdy loser I still saw in the mirror. I was an independent woman, full-on Destiny's Child–style.

I was no one's pining obsessive. I was a phoenix rising from the ash collected on the floor of my childhood home. I wanted to go back in time and hug middle school me and tell me everything was going to be, not just okay, but, amazing and awesome; that this crush was going to turn out better than I ever thought; that I deserved to be loved back.

After about ten minutes, I got up, put my clothes back on, and told him I had to go outside to make a phone call. Just like that. I was truly the powerful being Jessilyn and I had always pretended to be. The spell was indeed broken.

I grabbed my flip phone, stood in the empty hotel hallway, and pulled my long, sweaty hair back into a ponytail.

Then, I called Alex.

OUR SONGS: MONEY (MONEY)/(BONGOS)
Rebecca Loeser

When I was ten, I wrote songs. Once they were composed and edited to my liking, I'd select an appropriate demo track on my brother's Realistic Concertmate-670. Realistic was the RadioShack house brand. I'd record what were sure to be instant Billboard Hot 100 charters. They were all titled "Song" on a black plastic tape recorder, whose size and recording abilities both rivaled those of a five-pound Belgian waffle.

In one song, I wrote, "coda." I have no idea what this musical term means, but evidently ten-year-old Rebecca does.

The tape recorder was originally purchased for use in answering machines. But in my possession, it was a prospective star-making contraption with the power to propel me out of a school full of bullies and into the boom boxes—and hearts—of a nation.

Presented below are some abridged lyrics, copied from a spiral-bound notebook still in my possession.

December 31, 1998

Dear Journal,

So many celebrities died in 1998! Look: Shari Lewis, John F. Kennedy Jr., Florence Griffith Joyner, Sonny Bono. That's *nowhere near* half of them! There is about 3 dozen, no joke!

Song:

I could spend my li-ife / Mournin' over you / But then / There are / A lot of things / That I could doooo. / (Beat.) 'Cuz you never really died. / (Beat.) I keeeep you a-liiive / With the love inside. Oh-ho.

WITHOUT YOUR LOVE / Without your strength / I TELL YA HON I WOULD LOOOOSE / Without your love / Without your strength / I would never be the person that I ammmmmmm.

Song:

(Spoken.) I step out of my Limosine / I strut in my / gold shoes / an' I / show off my / thousand-dollar 'do / an' I feel good / as I walk with you. (Chorus.) Mmmmm but I'm not that type of material / girl in this / fast-paced world / with nothin' to lose / but a pair of shoes / Oh-ooooooo Oh-ooooooo

(Spoken.) I take a bite / of a cocktail wienie / an' I flirt / with the guys / an' bust my savings on a raffle ticket for / a trip for two / on a quiet romantic cruise / (Say.) ha more like expensive.

Oooo we only care (we only care) / 'bout our own sweet selves (yeah our own sweet selves) / Money (money) / Money (money) / (BONGOS.)

January 1, 1999

Song:

You're my best friend / and nothing says that / like the fact that you are alwaaaaaays therrrrre for meeeeee / You're my best friend / showing me the way / and I know we'll be together / until our last days.

Oh!

What is the meaning / Of a camera without film? / Or a spoon without a haaaandle? / Oh! / What is the meaning / of a person / without another person / to love her, / like her, / understand her / greatest sorrow?

January 2, 1999

'60s RULE!

[Rebecca's Note: *This is the only one with a title that's not "Song."*]

(Say.) Did it ever occur to / someone like you / that maybe they were wiser back then / (who knew) / (Sing.) Yaaaaohaaaa / Here is what I wish you would do: / Make love / Not war / (That's what we used to say and do!) / Helllll no, / I won't go / (My brothers disagree with war, too!) / Get out your signs / and your bell-bottoms too / (We'll just go out naked) / Now that makes me say (eeeew!)

(Chorus.) We're goin' back in time / To when PEACE / was not a crime / There was something called love, but today, we've forgotten / What friendship was, so I'm here to let you know (Ya!)

This is your own true time / To let your wild side shine / So forget about war / and forget about your trouble / Together we will learn about "good" / Hey hey hey! (Chorus again.) / Now we hope / you will practice this way / (It's cool!) / So now just say / ('60s RULE!) / 'cuz they do

January 5, 1999

Dear Journal,

Sorry I wrote all those songs. It's just that I made an album last night—with cool photos and everything! Right now I'm in Hebrew. The new year is good so far. I have to go.

Later, Babe.

NOT JUST A PHASE
Suzy X

At thirteen, I was different, but very confident. I had an active social life. I went on dates, kissed boys, joined Girl Scouts, and passed notes in which I often gossiped about other people's fashion choices. (I thought my fashion choices were far superior, although I'd beg to differ now.)

For those of us who were of the metal, punk, or gothic persuasion, the term *tortured soul* may come to mind when we think of ourselves in middle school. But I wouldn't call myself tortured; I just had a lot of hormones and an authority problem, always ready to throw my middle finger at anyone who crossed me.

In ninth grade, though, I arrived at the school talent show in a black tank top and bell-bottoms, covered in glow-in-the-dark stars. A black mesh cape draped from my shoulders and arms. My poem "Night" was a cliché to top all mall-goth clichés—it was about a mysterious woman clothed in shadows, Night, yearning for a handsome fellow known as Day. Of course, the following Monday at school, I was ridiculed by some upperclassmen in the hallway for being "the worst act ever."

But at twenty-three, I'm still floored by the gall of my response. "Hahaha! Jealous much?" I had asked as I gave them the finger and strutted away, leaving them speechless.

If I could talk to my thirteen-year-old self, I'd say: stay punk, and for Chrissakes, JUST DO YOUR HOMEWORK.

TRUTH OR DARE
Michael Greenwald

"Michael! Truth or dare? Michael! Truth or dare? Michael! Truth or dare truth or dare *truth or dare....*"

Most children stop playing the game of Truth or Dare around Bar-Mitzvah season. The members of Walt Whitman High School's Chamber Choir, however, play almost religiously.

Except, of course, for me.

On an afternoon that would become historically embarrassing, the Chamber Choir piled into the bus back to school after unleashing another epic concert at some faraway location. For a while, we felt content to simply lounge in our performance tuxedos, but eventually, the inevitable needed to occur.

"Truth or Dare?" Devon asked.

My friends nodded solemnly.

Feeling exhausted and not particularly interested in hearing about my friends' limited sexual escapades, I tried to decline. But they persisted.

"I'll just close my eyes and not even pay attention," I whined.

To not participate was ludicrous. After an endless period of pestering and prodding, I finally had to relent. Emma asked me something, I asked Justin something, the game continued. I thought that would appease my friends.

"Seriously, guys, I don't want to play."

"Just one more round, Michael! You have to play!"

"I DON'T WANT TO PLAY."

Every time, I caved. And every time, I felt myself becoming more and more irritated. No, not irritated. *Enraged*. I bottled my fury, but as my muscles tightened and bitter sweat cascaded down my body, I knew that I could not contain my anger for much longer.

My turn again. I was fighting on principle now.

"Michael, truth or dare?"

"I don't want to play."

"Michael, truth or dare?"

"Fuck! Truth."

"Who do you like?"

At the moment of this writing, the event in question occurred eight years ago. I am not trying to cover up an embarrassing crush or save myself from identifying someone on that bus. Eight years later, I would feel ready to admit that secret. I assure you, then, that I responded with complete and total honesty when I said . . .

"I don't know. I guess I don't really like anyone right now."

My friends went nuts. Howling like baboons at a baboon orgy, they screamed for an answer. "How could you not like anyone? Everyone likes at least *someone*. Come on, Michael! *Who do you like?*"

First, I didn't want to play. Then, when I did play, my answers were unacceptable. This game was un-winnable! Amazingly, I remained calm, but my insides were pounding like . . . baboons at a baboon orgy (damn, similes are *hard*).

"Fine, Michael," my friends finally decided, "just ask the next question."

Reader, if you have not yet absorbed this point, I will reiterate just one final time that I had absolutely no interest in this. Yet, being the clever and reasonable man that I am, I chose not to argue. I instead elected to ask a totally inane question to demonstrate the stupidity of this terrible excuse for amusement.

"Helen," I offered, "truth or dare?"

"Truth," she said.

"What's your favorite color?"

"I don't know," she said. "I guess I don't really have a favorite color."

Ha! Exactly my response for the "who do you like" question! My eyes darted amongst my friends, gleefully waiting for them to demand a real answer. But they all simply nodded.

"What the hell?" I seethed. "Don't you realize—"

"Michael, relax," said Devon. "It's just a game."

I saw red.

My muscles tightened, my heart twisted into a thumping fiery rage, I teetered on the brink of eruption. *Hopefully a considerate classmate would say something intelligent to soothe me!*

"Hey," observed Evan, who happened to be sitting next to me, by the window. "She kinda said the same thing as Michael. Isn't that funny?"

Match. Spark. Explosion. I'm pretty sure I blacked out, but my friends were kind enough to inform me of the series of events that followed.

I grabbed Evan by his tuxedo jacket and hurled him up against the bus window, slamming his body into the glass over and over again as I shrieked:

"DON'T!" (slam) "YOU!" (slam) "SEE!" (slam) "THE!" (slam) "*IRONY!*"

Then, I collapsed into his chest and wept.

Every person on that bus slowly turned to witness the unfolding meltdown. The entire Chamber Choir, my music teacher, a smattering of parent chaperones—they all stared in horror as this gangly high school student alternated between throwing his friend into a bus window and sobbing uncontrollably. No one moved. Evan laughed as I shook him, simultaneously fearing for his life and preparing to tell this story at lunch tomorrow.

"DON'T!" (slam) "YOU!" (slam) "SEE!" (slam) "THE!" (slam) "*IRONY!*"

I regained consciousness at a rest stop somewhere along the East Coast. The bus had pulled over, allowing everyone to take a much-needed breather. I sat alone on a bench, fidgeting with my bow tie.

Evan wandered over to me.

"You all right?" he asked.

At seventeen years old, I felt ashamed of my limited sexual experiences and my debilitating awkwardness around girls. Allowing myself to like anyone and then (God forbid!) admitting that interest to other people would create a terrifying pressure to overcome that awkwardness and actually *do* something. Bolstered by the clarity that follows a complete nervous breakdown, though, I realized that maybe it was time to not only embrace my awkward, but share it. There's got to be a girl out there as weird as me; I just never tried to look.

"I'm fine," I said to Evan, really meaning it. "I'm feeling much better."

"Let's get back on the bus then." Evan put his arm around me and smiled. "I want to play Never Have I Ever."

BEATER ON THE GRYFFODER QUIDDITCH TEAM

Claire Linic

September 22, 2000

Dear Bethany,

I bought you today at the book fair for 9 dollars you were defintty worth it. I will not be writing in you again until school starts at Hogwarts. I am so excited I am saving up my money for a firebolt I found the first one ever (I am the beater on the the Gryffoder Quidditch team). I have to find a really good place to hide you were no one will ever find you. I hope to see you soon

Sincerely,

Elizabether Turney (Claire Linic)

I was a Harry Potter fanatic. Countless hours were spent practicing my spells while drinking strawberry-peach Shasta. I even opened up a Hogwarts School of my own but kicked everyone out after one day. They were not taking anything seriously and just being real Hufflepuffy about it.

After writing this first entry in my new diary (Bethany, apparently), I hid it so well that it was lost for eleven years. I looked everywhere for it, but I could never remember the secret hiding place.

After I moved to Chicago, my parents brought me boxes of stuff from home. My long-lost journal was at the very top. I stand firmly by the fact this all happened through magic. Bethany was in the box of requirement and surfaced when I needed it most. It was amazing to get a reminder of the creative weirdo I was growing up. I have worked to remain that weirdo in my everyday life as ongoing celebration of the coolest kid I know—ten-year-old me.

NERD HERD
Kathleen Fitzgerald

Following years of public education, I entered Fort Worth, Texas's Nolan Catholic Junior High School as seventh grade's "cool public school girl." But this once-in-a-lifetime cool period—think *Saved by the Bell*'s Kelly Kapowski—abruptly ended when teachers discovered I'd already read *The Outsiders* and moved me to Advanced English, immediately torpedoing any chances I had at progressing past chicken-fighting with popular "It boy" Ryan Meed to below-the-shoulders sparring.

Luckily, amid the grammar diagrams and uninformed jokes about singing from diaphragms, I found a tribe of girls with whom I'd survive the next six years. We called ourselves The Nerd Herd. No one else called us this, because no one cared enough to notice.

There was Amanda: the countercultural Weezer fan. Bridget: "Reject #1," who never made a sports team . . . or made out with a boy. Katie: "Reject #2," similarly outcast by the ambiguously eastern European volleyball coach. Genesee: Backstreet Boy Nick Carter's tallest stalker. Christa: the cool one (thanks to boobs and a boyfriend). And me: someone who once unknowingly acted as a slumber-party human study guide for a friend who'd not yet completed our assigned reading. I was okay with it after realizing that her mom would pay for my All-You-Can-Eat-Chicken Fried Steak Feast at The Country Buffet the next morning.

The *only negative thing* I could say about these girls was how competitive they were with their grades, making *me* look relaxed. Me, the kid who at the age of nine couldn't sleep all night after watching the Greg Louganis biopic *Breaking the Surface*, because I was sure that I, too, had contracted pool-borne AIDS from Rolling Hills Country Club; who at eleven had a panic attack in a Limited Too dressing room because the hip *Newsies*-style cap on my head meant that I was getting older, and if *I* was getting older, my mom was aging, too, and "Holy sh*t, I'm gonna be a seventy-five-year-old orphan." But when it came to anything besides class ranking, these girls had my headgear'ed back.

Neurotically enough, The Nerd Herd found each other the way that all actual nerds do—by process of elimination. Separating the socially precocious from our unkempt chaff, we were thrilled finally to locate other girls who shared our individual fondness for Chick-fil-A nugget platters and extra credit.

While seventh-grade counterparts like "Born-Again-Christian Brie" did things in hot tubs that we still haven't tried today (the only thing that gets hot in my tubs is fried chicken), we were throwing super-cool, girls-only costume parties in our parents' homes.

Our parties rivaled Hugh Hefner's in both frequency and gender ratio—99 percent of attendees were girls; 1 percent were confused father figures accidentally walking past.

This tight, self-selecting "Delta 'tween Alphas & Betas" sorority was committed to grades, joint survival, and most importantly, our costumed alter egos. (When dressed as Celine Dion at that Pop Star

Exhibit A: DRESS-LIKE-A-FEMALE-IN-HISTORY PARTY

From L to R: Cleopatra, Maharani, Lady Godiva (clothed for winter), Holly Golightly
(adorned for 'stitution), Jacqueline Kennedy (dressed for assassination)

Exhibit B: DRESS-LIKE-A-POP-STAR PARTY
Katie/Reject#2 won this party for dressing like the Backstreet Boys' AJ McLean, complete with shot glass in honor of AJ's recent rehab stint.

Exhibit C: DRESS-LIKE-A-SPICE-GIRL "PARTY"*
(*15 percent party, 85 percent dance routine)
G is for Ginger; Blond is for Baby; Boa, Butterfly Clips, and Bonsai is for Ethnically Confused Spice.

party, I refused to speak for *two hours*, because I was certain that my "she-really-disappeared-into-the-role!" French-Canadian accent would give away everything before the group reveal.)

While cutthroat about GPA, The Nerd Herd found other ways to tourniquet friendships—whether creating boy band–themed get-well-soon cards ("Nick Lachey wants *you* to get back to 98(.6) Degrees soon."); voting one of us Blancas into the office of Spanish National Honor Society President; or sitting together in silence, in a dimly lit room, when a close friend of the Herd died.

There's power in numbers, and we were no exception. While ripe for teasing, we rarely received it to our faces. We never partied with booze or boys; instead we got buzzed off serving on school honor councils, using words like "dilapidated," and remaining willfully ignorant about our dance dates being either make-believe or closeted. In retrospect, a swirlie or two wouldn't have been far-fetched. But there were six of us. And only four toilets in each of our school's bathrooms. Besides, people instinctively know not to mess with a group of nerds too much in case Future You ever needs a lawyer (which two now are), amnesty grant (one has connections), or doctor (we choked there).

For more than two thousand school days, we stood shoulder-to-shoulder in the social battlefield of junior high and high school. Between pretending to be pop stars and historical figures, we were there—there to learn, there to cover our test answers like we were protecting the nuclear codes, there to try things solo, there to fail, there to survive.

As a word, *survival* is total cheeseballs. As an anagram, it's perfect: *via lurvs*—translating to "life loves" or "through love."

Today, these lifelong loves dot the US countryside: BSB Stalker is working as an educator in Oregon; Reject #1 has found international acceptance in the US State Department; Reject #2 is putting away bad guys in the Boston District Attorney's Office; The Cool One is a lawyer in Texas (still has the boobs and now a lifelong boyfriend, a.k.a husband); countercultural Weezer fan is a Texas sales executive, married and pregnant with her first child; and The Human Study Guide lives in Chicago, an accidental technologist after aging out of the tutoring-for-fried-steak industry.

But, no matter what we do for work, how far we trek, how much we grow (emotionally *and* girth-wise), or how many years we put between us and the pheromonal battlefields of Fort Worth, Texas . . .

. . . once a Nerd Herd, always a Nerd Herd.

From L to R: Nerds

PEACEFUL OBLIVION
David Meyer

I am the young lad on the left thinking, *That older girl must think I am pretty cool to ask me to do this for her.* My older cousin—the one on the right—is probably thinking, *I can't believe they talked me into this.* This photo is just the tip of the awkward iceberg.

- I thought I must be very special when I was the only boy in the band who got to play his sister's hand-me-down clarinet.
- I thought I must be some dancer when they asked me to sing softer in swing choir and concentrate on my dance moves.
- I thought it was very perceptive of the band teacher when he asked me to videotape the band instead of actually be on the field during marching competition.

Looking back on it, this oblivion had its advantages. It taught me to play to my strengths and not worry about what I was not doing. And by the way, being the only boy in the clarinet section in the eleventh grade was not nearly as bad as it was in sixth grade.

However, as I type this, I think back to a recent conversation at work when my boss said, "David, we really like your input on this team, but there is a new team that really needs you instead." I guess I'm still playing to my strengths.

Jessica Stopak

Chapter 3

Fashion Icons

PHOTO BOOTH GIRL
Ashley England

Getting ready in 1999 as a fourteen-year-old high school freshman meant a lot of preparation. I wore evenly spaced butterfly clips and displayed the necklace that Drew Barrymore wore in *The Wedding Singer* prominently over my American Eagle men's sweater. My chubby fingers would tighten my size-twelve AE jeans as I would step into Doc Martens with the Union Jack flag on the toes. Everything I put on, I put on for me. I thought I looked cool, and moreover, I felt cool.

I wasn't interested in boys. I carried a book of Beatles chords around like the Bible. I ate melted cheddar cheese out of a coffee mug as a snack every day after school. I didn't care about the *now*, because I wanted to be famous. I was just living this life until my real, famous life started.

When I was alone, I would narrate my actions to an imaginary camera. I would do accents and sing and laugh about how charming and funny and famous I was. I watched *The Rosie O'Donnell Show* religiously, carrying on fake interviews with her in my living room during the commercial breaks. I practiced entering the imaginary set from the foyer because I wanted to be prepared for when I was on her show. Every night, I fell asleep thinking about how I would be famous, imagining myself meeting other famous people, singing songs in front of massive crowds, walking red carpets. In public, I would walk around with my head down, practicing not being recognized. I knew what I had inside, and I was just waiting for it to come out.

But I lost her.

I started to care about what other people thought. I began to question my taste, what I thought was cool, what I should be eating and wearing and thinking. I looked to others instead of to myself.

I've worked for years to find that girl in the photo booth. You might think she looks ridiculous, but she was really cool. I wish I hadn't lost touch with her, because she knew me the best, and she really had it going on.

A LETTER TO THE MALL KIDZ
Tyler Gillespie

*H*ey, *Mall Kid*.

You have just choreographed a dance to *NSYNC's "Digital Get Down," and you are taking a glamour shot in the middle of a Florida mall. I'd say, you're making stellar life choices right now. You wonder, though, about post-mall life, and I'm here to tell you there is one. It's filled with love and heartbreak and big, adult decisions. But don't worry, you will still secretly love the mall and will always be able to do some moves from the *NSYNC routine, if prompted.

Now, as the ghost of Mall Kid Past, I have to tell you some bad news. There will be a time when you look back at this picture and get embarrassed because you are *just trying so hard*. Florida, why are you wearing a Detroit baseball hat when 1) you know your head is too big for a hat, and 2) you aren't Eminem? The two chains, middle school basketball shirt, and, really, the Tommy lanyard? Your look feels contrived, like this is how you think you're *supposed* to dress. You will never, ever, ever want to show this photo to anyone, and you will consider ripping it up. I mean, *seriously*.

But here's what I need you to know: you look good in front of that palm-tree background, and this is actually one of your best photos. Your grandparents took you to the mall for this picture because you didn't like your class photo. You felt the school picture wasn't *you*. Remember: your family always supported you—even in wearing an all-navy, shimmery-blue outfit. Remember: your uncle bought you stacks of JNCO jeans so you'd feel cool. Remember: every year your mom took you to get new school shirts no matter how slow it was at the restaurant. Bad fashion with good intentions.

Mall Kid—if I can be frank for a minute—I know why you tried so hard, and it's okay for you to still be figuring stuff out. Breathe—it really is okay. Your Southern Baptist Christian high school has made you sign a "morality contract," which states you won't participate in any "secular activities," the very worst of all, GAY THOUGHTS. I feel for you so hard right now, because you still have nearly two years left of worrying they'll find out and you'll get expelled and never get into college. You have two years left of wearing all-navy-blue outfits. I feel tears starting to well up right now—not for the navy blue, it's actually a good color—but because things are going to get rough for you in the next few years. It's going to knock the wind out of you. You are going to make some really bad choices—this outfit won't even count as a top-fifty mistake.

You will forget who you wanted to be. You will forget to laugh. You will forget to take the time to take care of yourself and the people you love.

But, Mall Kid, in this time, you will go on plenty of JOURNEYS and you won't stay FOREVER 21, which is a good thing because VICTORIA'S SECRET is this: you were meant to be a true AMERICAN EAGLE.

My point, Mall Kid, is this: *you will learn to laugh at yourself*—your somewhat bad pop culture jokes, the way you slouch, your teeth (which you've always hated). You will learn that loving yourself is laughing at yourself; it's forgiveness. You will spend a few years making up for lost laugh-time. Maybe you will spend your whole life. You are laughing right now, because you think it's so deep and weird to say laughing at yourself is a form of forgiving yourself. But, you believe it, because maybe it is.

You feel good right now, and you don't want to tell yourself this last thing you have to tell yourself. You are stalling. Remember: "Digital Get Down." Okay, you can do this.

This is the ghost of Mall Kid Future talking now, and I'm contractually obligated to tell you that you forget to laugh at yourself again. Then, relearn. Remember. Then, forget. Relearn. You start to believe your whole life will look like this process because we grow and have to take the time to learn about ourselves.

Mall Kid past, present, and future, if you remember nothing else or have been "like, whatever" this whole time, LISTEN UP. Always take the time to learn about yourself and please laugh (forgiveness) and try your best to make other people feel like it's okay to laugh at themselves, because IT IS.

It is—it really, really is. It, also, is what it is. [Laugh at yourself.]

Now, go have fun and turn your Tommy lanyard in at the front desk—you won't need it anymore where you're going.

Your Friend,

Ghost of Mall Kid Present, or, as Mom still calls us, *Ty*

GRANDMA BRAS BY THIRTEEN
Sylvia Miller

I magine a group of teenage girls talking as they walk to class. Me, I'm trailing behind just enough that I am not actually part of the conversation, but close enough I can hear all that's being said.

"We should all have a cleavage competition," Riley declares. "You know, see who has the biggest cleavage! Except you, Sylvia. You can't compete, because we all know you would automatically win."

Yes, my boobs have been big since junior high. I know, I know, I've heard it a million times: *Your boyfriend/husband will love them. Every girl will be so jealous of you!* But let me tell you, having the same size melons as Dolly Parton at thirteen only makes junior high and high school places of eternal embarrassment.

I remember walking through the lingerie aisles looking at all the pink and purple bras with flowers or unicorns on them and heading straight for the boxed grandma bras. Mind you, these bras didn't really fit, either. I just wore them like a big ACE bandage wrapped around my bosom. I'd try them on, usually a size D, jump around a bit to make sure nothing moved, and voilà! Bound boobies. To ensure no one ever saw the embarrassingly beige bras, I never changed in the locker room or at sleepovers.

In high school, the baby tees had just regained popularity. My oversized knockers and I were not missing out on this trend. I spent about three years of my life squeezing my tatas into tiny tees and tugging the always too-short shirts down to meet my low-rise jeans. Two bras

were necessary to participate in gym and to play softball. The elastic was always wearing thin and giving out and the straps were always digging into my shoulders, begging to be released. The poor things would never last very long. I even snapped a bra during a cheerleading routine—twice.

My huge hooters continued to annoy, embarrass, and cause both mental and psychological damage throughout my high school career. Then came the thing I had been dreading for years: junior prom. If you haven't noticed, they do *not* make prom dresses in which you can wear a bra with straps—hung honkers' worst nightmare. After being told that I was "too big" and needed "specially designed bras" by the women at Victoria's Secret, my mom took me to a lingerie store where the woman took one look at me and said, "Honey, you're at *least* an F." Now, for those laymen out there, bra sizes are A, B, C, D, DD, DDD, and then me at sixteen, F. And a bit of review: I was squeezing my ginormous jugs into a D. I tried on an F-cup bra and was almost in tears at how wonderfully it fit. No longer were my voluptuous ladies flattened to pancakes, but rather, they were lifted, separated, and supported. I got two bras that day: one strapless for prom and one that I wore every day for the next year.

I took all of my big-boobed friends to this wonderful shop so they too could have their Come-to-Jesus moment. I became an evangelist of good bras. I couldn't stop talking about how a bra that fits can change your world like it did mine! All you have to do is open yourself up to the possibility and let the bra come into your life. Accept it as your own personal back savior!

This moment in the dressing room with a complete stranger helping me fasten a bra and making sure everything was in the right place was the first step for me to accept me and my body. I no longer thought of my boobs as something for a theoretical husband somewhere down the line; they were mine. They were for me. I like my boobs. They made me look complete, beautiful, and sexy. My boobs and I have been through many ups and downs (finding that perfect sports bra did take a bit longer), but I have become completely comfortable with their size.

And yes, *Riley*, I would still win at a cleavage competition.

ANNIE, GET YOUR BRACES
Allison Sinclair

During the early nineties, my older brother called me Buck because of my severe overbite. Being made fun of by a sibling is probably normal, but I felt extremely embarrassed by his name-calling. This sibling squabble felt worse, because my peers, too, made fun of my teeth. In a defensive response to a name-calling classmate, I said, "I can fix my teeth but you can't fix your face." Not

my best moment, but my retort did stop him from making fun of me.

My wonderful parents were proactive and got me braces as soon as possible. My hardware may have cost a lot of money, but my parents overlooked the financial burden it put on the family. But my brace-face stopped my smile for two long years. I didn't want to show my braces so I tried to hide my teeth in pictures. Thankfully, my braces were taken off in time for high school.

My vision issues, though, popped up, too. In the car with my mother, I looked out to a cornfield—we were living in Nebraska—and asked, "Why is there a house in the middle of a cornfield?" Turns out, there was no house. It was a grain truck. Crap, my luck! Contacts weren't an option due to my young age and lack of responsibility. Lasik surgery hadn't been invented yet. The only option was to wear big, bulking glasses that covered up my entire face. On top of having red hair and buckteeth, I now had glasses. I thought things just simply couldn't get any worse.

As a girl born with strawberry-blond hair, my parents were great at providing me with redheaded dolls, and the movie *Annie* normalized the rare hair color for me. My hair color didn't bother me like it did other kids my age. With all this, I constantly felt judged, but I tried to remember, *Love thy neighbor as thyself*. All of my fixable issues sorted themselves out over time, and I eventually evolved into who I am today: a walking replica of my mother. And that's a good thing!

A PAIR OF JANE GOODALL KHAKIS
Shannon Noll

Hey, you. You with the stirrup stretch pants. You don't have to smile. We all know you hate that tutu. Sure, pretending you like it might make your mom happy for a day. But guess what? If you keep up with this act, she's only going to buy you more.

You remember that time you opened up a present, and it was a box that had once held furnace filters? You declared, *Just what I always wanted*, because that's what they say in movies. Did you really want furnace filters, or were you just trying to make someone happy? This is kind of like that.

When your cousins come to visit in the spring, that cheerful little pixie next to you will dress your boy cousin in the same getup. Only people won't say he's pretty or adorable; they will joke and laugh. You will wonder why, especially since you felt just as ridiculous wearing it as he looks. People can't always see what's inside unless you tell them.

You don't know this yet, and in fact, you won't let yourself know this for nearly two more decades, but you are queer. And you're in good company, because so is your tutu-loving sister. You are both totally queer-balls, each in your own way. Don't let fear hold you back from that revelation for so long. It's okay. Fear is a part of the journey, but on the other side is the kind of joy that will fill the hole you feel inside you. It will allow you to stop freaking out your mom by asking things like "Who am I?" while she's trying to make dinner.

Going with the flow like you are, spending your effort on trying to please others over yourself, that's going to get you in trouble down the road. So, do yourself a favor, thank Mom for that tutu, crown, and scepter, then firmly declare that you want a set of Jane Goodall khakis.

THEN, HIGH SCHOOL HAPPENED
Ryann Bird

W ho is the fabulous child, and why is she dressed like that?

Well it was ten-year-old me, and probably because it was a Tuesday.

When I was little, I was the spunkiest, most original, and confident child anyone had ever met. I wore what I wanted—often old prom dresses, crocheted shirts, or just a swimsuit. I always

tried to make my hair as Disney Channel's *Lizzie McGuire*-esque as possible. I put on concerts and made all of my neighbors and friends come to them. I created beautiful and creative works of art. I climbed trees and helped all my friends learn how to build the best tree forts. I was 120 percent, genuinely happy.

Then, high school happened.

I moved from my beloved country-school to the town high school and a whole group of people who, while I had known them my whole life, were WAY too cool for the little-kid stuff I still enjoyed. Within a matter of months, those mean girls and boys managed to fully extinguish the multicolored flame that was my personality. I quit singing, dancing, and painting. I was often blamed for things I didn't do. Girls would berate me in the halls or forbid me to join them for lunch.

To combat this, I threw myself into as many academic activities as possible, and I became the girl who had it together. I organized chili-feeds, fund-raisers, school dances, anything to keep my mind off the fact that I was not me anymore. Senior year, I was the president of math club, the senior class, student government, FBLA, National Honors Society, and involved in many other clubs. All to get into a college and GET AWAY!

Good news: I went to college. But it started off rough.

I didn't trust girls and assumed most of the guys were jerks. Guess what? I made some friends, though, and these friends enjoyed my "flaws." They encouraged me to be myself. They liked that I sang all the time, and I even started to get my sense of humor back.

I learned that real friendships between women can exist. There is no competition, no belittling, no pain. There is laughter, shoulders to cry on, and a support system that is solid. Oh, and constant singing.

MALL GOTH
Suzy Exposito

Halloween 2001 was the beginning of a crucial turning point in my life: the point at which I began cultivating my punk identity. Halloween was the ideal time to start my evolution, when regular pharmacies and department stores were suddenly abundant with cheap black lipsticks and spiked dog collars.

During the late-nineties' reign of clean-cut Disney pop stars, I was secretly enjoying the sounds of Nirvana and Green Day. But without anyone to share these things with, I felt the urgency to quit being a nerd and bond with the "alternative" kids at my middle school. It was time to take the full plunge into punk rock.

It was during a fated trip to the mall that I realized the potential this holiday had. My mom, sister, and I were scanning the aisles of the Halloween store for costume ideas. I had on a regular old shirt from Old Navy (as pictured) that said, "I ROCK!" Earlier that day, in class, some cheerleader who very closely resembled Miss Piggy sneered, "You rock? Yeah, right."

I had just scowled at her. But I decided that this Halloween, I would affirm who I truly was on the inside—I told my mom I wanted a Rocker Chick "costume" for Halloween. And so we bought a pair of black fishnets, safety pins, jelly bracelets, and lavender hair extensions. Later on, we stopped by the Army Navy store to find some *real* combat boots in my size. My little sister rolled her eyes and groaned to my mom, "You know she's just making you buy that stuff so she can wear it every day." My mom simply shrugged and said, "Pick a costume and let's get out of here."

As my little sister resentfully predicted, I started wearing miniskirts, fishnets, and combat boots regularly, well into the eleventh grade. And over ten years later, the teen punk is still in me when I sing with my band on stage or when I come to work in a cut-up band shirt under my pastel cardigan. I will never forget her.

I'LL ALWAYS BE AN AMERICAN GIRL DOLL
Marie Maloney

What exactly makes people become who they are? Would we always have become the people we are even if our life circumstances were different? I don't think anyone truly has the answers to these questions, but I've come to the solid conclusion that part of the reason I am the person I am today is because, as a child, I was dressed like an American Girl doll.

Before I was born, my parents were having trouble conceiving, and my mom desperately wanted a child. I've been told she went and saw *Three Men and a Baby* in the theater multiple times and sobbed uncontrollably through each screening. She was getting steal-a-baby desperate when they were chosen to be my adoptive parents, and finally all was right in her world. In 1988, American Girl dolls weren't exactly en vogue, so I don't think the clothing choice started out as intentional. Yet as I grew into more of a small person, the doll-like dressing continued, and I encouraged it! In the winter, my mom would try to get me to wear pants to shield my skinny chicken legs from the cold, and I would throw the jeans back at her, demanding my dress. I refused to wear trousers of any kind, and my dresses had to have the paramount quality of flaring out when I twirled. Meaning, I would stand in department store changing rooms at five years old and do the Twirl Test on each dress I tried on. Talk about a diva!

Most American Girl dolls have a historical backstory to them. The American Girl I looked and dressed most like was the fanciest of all American Girl dolls, Samantha, from the Victorian era. While most girls my age were rocking light-up LA Gears and whitewash jeans, I was rolling up to school in pleated dresses with Peter Pan collars. My outfits had themes, too. One outfit, I still remember to this day, was a navy blue dress that had gold

anchor buttons down the middle. I paired this with white frilly socks and navy two-tone hush puppies, and I was ready for adventure on the high seas of Mokena, Illinois. As my dad dropped me off at preschool in this outfit, my farewell to him was: "Do I look like a sailor or what?!"

Did my parents mold me into this American Girl, or was I just born this way? I can't help but feel that my fondness for dressing up is just intrinsically linked to my personality. I simply can't help it. For better or worse, no matter how old I get, I think deep down I'll always be an American Girl.

When I was growing up, I had always wanted Zack Morris's (of *Saved by the Bell*) hair. Unfortunately for me, I had Screech's hair type. That didn't stop me, though! At the end of eighth grade, I shaved the sides of my head and bleached my curly locks.

—Spensaur Cooper

Chapter 4

Growing Pains

VOLLEYBALL AND MY FUNERAL LEOTARD
Dawn Luebbe

As a six-foot-two adult, one of the first things people ask me is if I ever played volleyball. It's a logical question to which the short answer is *yes*. However, the term of my athletic prowess lasted a mere one week and inadvertently left me in crisis counseling with our middle school guidance counselor.

As an abnormally tall preteen, the volleyball team seemed like the perfect place for me. Our science teacher, Ms. D, who also happened to be the coach, had even recruited me herself. I soon convinced myself that in no time I'd be the star of the team, strutting down the hallways of Pound Middle School wearing sunglasses and signing autographs with my Squiggle Wiggle Writer pen.

At this point, I should probably note that I wasn't exactly athletic. The closest thing to a sport I had participated in was jazz dance classes. My only knowledge of volleyball came from watching the Malibu Beach Club episodes of *Saved by the Bell*. But if Jessie Spano could be a star striker, so could I.

I strutted into the gym on the first day of practice ready to dominate in my Umbros and No Fear T-shirt. Ms. D gave us a pep talk and then instructed us to run laps as a warm-up. I tightened the laces of my LA Gears and started sprinting. Perhaps it was because I had practically no experience running or maybe it was because my usual after-school activities involved watching *Clarissa Explains It All* and eating Keebler Fudge Sticks, but after half a lap, I was exhausted. I half-limped and wheezed my way through the rest of the warm-up and, despite the logo on my T-shirt, I started to get scared.

The next couple practices progressed pretty much in the same manner. When I managed to make contact with the volleyball, it stung my hands in an unpleasant way, and the ball never really went where I wanted it to. The only reason I didn't quit was because my friend Renee was on the team. Renee was super cool and lived on a horse farm, and I figured if we became better friends, I would be invited to her farm to go riding.

I previously mentioned my participation in jazz dance classes. I devoutly went every Thursday after school to Cabbage Patch and Roger Rabbit my way through En Vogue classics. I had known all week that I would have to leave volleyball practice early on Thursday to make it to dance on time. However, I was terrified to break this news to Ms. D, who I knew would not be happy with me missing practice given my lackluster volleyball skills.

Thursday got closer and closer, and I still had not told Ms. D that I needed to leave early. All of a sudden, Thursday was here, and as I struggled through practice, I kept looking at the clock, trying to find the right moment to tell Ms. D I had to leave at 4:00. But whenever she came near, I clammed up. Soon the clock struck 4:00, and I still had not told her. I became overwhelmed with fear, and I decided the best thing to do would be to make a run for it.

Engaged in a full rally mid-court, I waited for the ball to drop and sprinted toward the door. I made it to the hallway and kept running. Soon, heart pounding, I was in the locker room, convinced that no one had noticed my stealthy exit.

Filled with nervous excitement, I quickly changed into my hot-pink spandex leotard. But just as I was pulling up the final strap and heading toward the door, in walked Ms. D. My stomach dropped, and I fully panicked. In a calm voice, but with a confused look as she eyed my leotard, Ms. D asked if everything was all right. Overcome with fear and shame, I burst into tears.

Ms. D tried to calm me and asked me what was going on. Through my uncontrollable sobbing and gasping for breath, I blurted out the only thing I could think of to justify my bizarre behavior.

"My cousin died."

As soon as I said it, I knew there was no going back.

With a pained look on her face, Ms. D asked how she died. I caught my breath and mumbled, "She was hit by a drunk driver." As a recent DARE graduate, I was confident this was the most believable, albeit most shameful, response. Ms. D started to ask follow-up questions, but I had to get out of there as soon as possible. Wiping my tears, I gasped, "I have to leave now to get to her funeral."

Looking back, I wonder why she didn't question me further—Why had I come to practice at all? Where were my parents? Why did I think a pink leotard was appropriate funeral attire? Luckily she let me leave, and I rushed off to jazz class.

The next day, I went to school feeling a little guilty, but mostly calm, knowing it would be smooth sailing (well, at least until next Thursday). I was sitting in English class, engrossed in *Hatchet*, when my teacher brought me a note. It was a pass to report to the school guidance counselor. Filled with dread, I slowly picked up my JanSport backpack and trudged to the counselor's office.

Sharon, the counselor, in her big red Sally Jessy Raphael glasses, spent the next hour asking me all about my cousin, her death, and talking about the horrible consequences of drunk driving. At no point did I confess to my horrible and pathetic lie. Instead, I elaborated on the story, providing more details about the crash and the funeral (there were bouquets of sunflowers—her favorite).

I was in deep.

After school that day, I went to volleyball practice. I suited up, but I knew volleyball just wasn't for me. I couldn't handle the physical and emotional distress. I slowly sulked over to Ms. D and told her I was quitting the team. She asked why I was leaving. I looked her in the eye and for a moment thought about telling the truth or maybe even a different truth: I sucked at volleyball.

But instead, my eyes welled with tears and I said, "I really need to be with my family during this difficult time."

And she understood.

A small part of me still feels guilty about this lie, the unnecessary concern I caused Ms. D, and having killed my imaginary cousin. I'd like to think I would act differently today as a somewhat less anxious person; however, I am still known to tell a ridiculous lie on occasion to avoid confrontation. I'd like to think I've at least gotten savvier in my lying, though. At least I no longer tell people I am on my way to a funeral in a leotard.

I WAS A POSER

Danny Bergman

Is it surprising that anyone survives middle school? Back in my day and hometown in Nebraska, we called it "junior high," and it was just as deadly.

Growth spurts, fashion sense, personal grooming—or a lack of all three. I was in seventh grade and struggling to let go of my Legos and G.I. Joes.

Still, I also knew changes were a-coming, and it was time to grow up. Everyone else

was attacking adolescence head-on, while I remained a head shorter than the rest of my peers. Since I couldn't wait for my body to catch up with my classmates', I had to outflank them armed with a snappy wardrobe and "style."

Drawing the line at Guess jeans, I clung to my Levi's and whatever brand names I could find at TJ Maxx and the Half-Price Store. To separate myself from the standard insignia-spotted sportswear look, I assumed the only other cool subculture—skaters. Vision Street Wear,

Vans, and Ocean Pacific gear filled my closet. Never mind that I lived at the most geographically distant point from either coast.

And never mind that I didn't actually own a skateboard. Not unless you count the pencil-thin plastic hand-me-down I scrounged from my grandparents' garage. Not that it would matter. Even if I possessed Tony Hawk's best board, I would've flailed off it like an epileptic jellyfish. I'd like to blame my prepubescent physiology for having zero skillz, but I'm probably just as incompetent today.

That's right. I was a "poser."

But it was junior high. Weren't we all posers then? This is my class photo from those days, featuring my floppy skater-do I shaved off a few months later to assume the preppy look and dive thumbs-first into Nintendo World.

And guess what? I was actually good at video games. (Probably because I had spent considerable time in the developmental Atari league during my grade school years. And those glasses enhanced my hand-eye coordination.)

My hair has stayed short for the rest of my life—with the exception of a rebellious/lazy shaggy phase a few years before I met my wife. And my toes haven't touched a skateboard in decades. But I still dig out my dusty NES from time to time to vanquish the evils of Bowser, Dr. Wily, and my wife's sense of humor.

We can all laugh now.

SPINNERS
Lucy Waters

Positioned artfully in my parents' driveway, between our skewed plastic mailbox and the rusted electrical post, my sparkly pink dress and cemented curls leave no question that I am ready for some princess-inspired festivities.

It took many pep talks to get me into that dress, a lot of encouragement to drag me out of the house, and all the love in the world to make light of a dramatic situation.

Before the accident, I was focused on achieving what all the glittery picture frames had promised: "The Best Senior Year EVER!" A year that promised spring break in Florida, hosting the talent show, and performing in our school's play. It was all set, all planned—until I was late for physics class.

Physics was my first class of the day and, shock to no one, I had finally received my third tardy, leveling up to the threat of detention. The very next morning, I was running behind, again. Instead of changing my behavior to avoid being late or accepting responsibility and serving detention, I thought it wiser to drive fast—really, really fast.

That icy March morning, I sped down a tree-lined Michigan back road and came upon a sensible sports utility vehicle. I moved to pass, and I hit a patch of black ice. My car spun out of control, and I collided head-on with a very sturdy tree.

My car was totaled, but luckily I wasn't.

I had shattered both my ankles and torn my ACL. I had a nasty bump on the head but no signs of brain damage (I've always been a bit odd, though, so how sure can you really be?). After a handful of surgeries, thirteen screws, and three weeks in the hospital, I was told I would walk again, but not before the end of the school year.

I was crushed, literally and figuratively.

My mother (a five-foot British firecracker) slept by my side every night I was in the hospital. Together we took midnight trips to the vending machines. She was my partner in crime. I have no idea how she put up with it all, but I am forever grateful that she did.

As high school continued on without me, I couldn't help but feel like my perfect senior year was gone. I would not be in the talent show or go on spring break and, worst of all, I would miss prom.

I had always pictured my high school experience as something close to what I had seen on TV and in movies. But now it seemed I would never have my own montage of shopping sprees and under-age drinking parties like Marissa Cooper. I would never embody the spirit of Cher Horowitz through a rich collection of kneesocks. I would never be greeted at the train station escalator by Ryan Phillippe and the Counting Crows.

There ain't no pity party like a seventeen-year-old-girl pity party, and this pity party had a Dashboard Confessional sound track. By the time my sulking hit critical mass, my friends were allowed to come visit.

While hospital living has its downsides (i.e., awkward encounters with roommates after Morphine Lucy referred to them as "uggos"), it does provide a captive audience and plenty of mind-tickling pain-killers. Soon I was "holding court" for my friends (as my mom had put it), and we were finally able to start making fun of the situation in which I had landed.

After I left the hospital, most of my home therapy consisted of me strapped to a loud machine that made my legs extend and contract as the bones and muscles grew stronger. As a result, my wardrobe was limited to cutoff pants. Cutoffs were the worst enemy to my body type, according to an infographic in *Seventeen* magazine.

One day, my friend Kate bought me the coolest red ADIDAS breakaway pants to accommodate my cast boots, and I started feeling more comfortable with the recovery process ahead. We laughed about the horror of not going shoe shopping for months. We joked that the wheelchair I was riding was actually another fashion accessory. Hip with the pop culture references, I suggested I should get spinning hubcaps and "pimp my ride."

A few months into my recovery, I was able to return to school. With the urging of the most loving family and friends in the world, I plucked up the courage to go to prom.

My mom helped me in and out of fitting rooms and hundreds of dresses before we chose the pinkest and most sparkly dress we could find. When it came time for accessories, I was bummed I wouldn't be able to wear ridiculous high heels (I would have fallen on my face, but they would've looked fantastic).

As my mom pushed me around Walmart one afternoon, suddenly she experienced a styling epiphany. She took me to the auto department and bought me a set of plastic spinning hubcaps and a can of pink spray paint.

Prom night finally arrived. Regularly, being driven to the dance by my mom and dad would have been mortifying, but it was comforting to wave to them as I wheeled into the prom.

The tired elevator doors creaked open. It was beautiful. I was stunned by the deafening bass of Usher and rogue sparkles of a beaten disco ball. The erratic laser lights made my classmates look like extras in a classy MTV dance special. The venue felt like a Moroccan nightclub. The air was an innocuous mixture of AF cologne and cheap liquor (Burnett's girls say, *Woo!*).

I edged around the undulating crowd to seek refuge by the refreshments. However, I didn't account for how conspicuous pink spinners would be. I was greeted with the warmest welcome. Everyone I passed smiled or offered a high five, and my anxiety melted away with the dry ice.

Seeing that I was avoiding it, Kate took me on a whirlwind tour of the dance floor. Everyone we passed danced with us; it felt like Carnival, with slightly more clothing. I even got a lap dance from one of dem popular boys!

As the prom wound down, I made my way back to the elevator. I passed a guy I had been crushing on since seventh grade. I was 95 percent certain he didn't know my full name. He saw me and left his very pretty freshman date to walk over. He leaned down, and I could smell the carnation on his lapel. It smelled like Axe.

He whispered, "You look beautiful."

My stomach turned inside out and filled with pins and needles. "Thanks. Dude. You look beautiful, too," I sputtered all over his shiny vest. He walked back to his date. I hit the elevator button feverishly a thousand times, smiling from ear to ear.

My prom experience was not the night I had imagined, but with the support of my friends and family, it was better. Leaving the dance floor, I felt exhilarated by the realization that when you accept an event or moment will never be perfect, you relieve all pressure to make it so. I felt more beautiful than Marissa Cooper, more fashionable than Cher Horowitz, and more popular than the Counting Crows. And in the end, my mother taught me the best lesson of my adolescence: sometimes you can conjure all the confidence and courage you need with a set of plastic hubcaps and a can of pink spray paint.

JUST HORSING AROUND
Edie Talley

Lucky snorted and stamped impatiently. I adjusted my boots in the stirrups, leaned forward, and then prodded his ribs with my heels. We entered the arena to the sound of a roaring crowd. Lucky's thundering hooves kicked up dirt clods that pummeled the ground behind us as we raced toward the black plastic barrel, open on both ends, lying on its side about two hundred feet ahead. When we reached it, I reined up hard and jumped off. I dropped to my belly and scurried through the barrel like a spider in a drain. So far, so good. I hopped up and ran, breathing hard, toward the beloved animal who helped me survive my awkward teenage years. Surprisingly, Lucky shied away, forcing me to chase him. I barely managed to grab the reins and get my left foot into the stirrup before he took off.

Just then, the only thing I cared more about than winning was looking good when I did it. Fat chance of that! Lucky rounded the barrel and headed out of the arena even faster than he'd entered it. I clutched the horn of the saddle and hung comically from one stirrup. In an effort to get properly seated, I somehow bounced right over Lucky's back and landed, face up, in the dirt.

The wildly cheering crowd became eerily silent when I went airborne. The heavy thud of my landing and the loud "ugh" of air being knocked from my lungs passed, unnoticed, into the warm Saturday night ether. The crowd heard the sound of every single snap on the front of my shirt separating like the firing of a machine gun. *Brrrraaaap!* It was sensational!

In those days, I was a self-conscious teenager who'd taken pains to dress carefully for the horse show—boots, jeans, a leather belt with a huge brass buckle, and a gorgeous Western shirt studded with pearl-covered snaps. Those beautiful snaps had undone me, literally. I was mortified to find myself sitting in the middle of the arena with my shirt splayed open, a silent, staring crowd surrounding me, and my horse running away like his ass was on fire. I didn't blame Lucky. I wanted to run, too.

Then someone in the crowd broke the spell. "Look!" he shouted, pointing at my exposed chest. Soon, others joined in. I hastily re-snapped my shirt to the sound of raucous laughter.

It might have been my most humiliating moment, except, suddenly it wasn't.

Finally, I mustered the courage to stand. My face was red, but I held my head high as I turned to walk out of the arena. Then I heard it: applause. It was the warm, heroic applause reserved for stunned quarterbacks who rise and walk off the field unaided, for figure skaters who finish their routines after hitting the ice.

In that magical moment, I learned victory takes many forms and I learned to accept it gracefully however it appears.

THE YEARBOOK PHOTO
Kenneth Soltis

Before I entered the eighth grade, doctors diagnosed me with an autoimmune disorder and prescribed multiple cycles of steroids as a treatment. The steroids proved effective, but the side effects included weight gain from an insatiable appetite, jacked-up acne, and above-average water retention. These are never particularly desirable traits, but they were especially dreadful in middle school, when my looks suddenly became important.

Years later, unhappy as an adult, I turned to therapy. On a couch in a cozy office, my body image came up, and I told the therapist I felt ugly. She disagreed, but I wouldn't hear it. When I looked in mirrors, my adult face was lean and pimple free, yet the memory of my plump, blemished adolescent face shrouded my reflection like a superimposed veil. I told the therapist about my yearbook photo from the eighth grade, and she wanted to see it. The yearbook was buried in a closet like a damning piece of evidence. I dug it out and brought it to the next session, where I flipped to the offending page and, with jittery hands, passed the book to her. My eyes bored into her face as she looked down at the photo, but I saw no flickers of disgust. The woman only smiled. "He's just a cute little boy," she said.

She handed the yearbook back to me, and the picture's context changed ever so slightly. I examined the photos near mine. She was right. My peers were children, most of them gawky in some way. I still didn't buy the therapist's gracious assessment of my photo. I thought her reaction was a therapeutic mind trick. Later, I showed the photo to friends, and their reactions bewildered me. Many of them found the boy in the photo adorable, and the picture changed again. I realized that my opinion of the picture was distorted. Ultimately, I understood that the body image I formed as a teenager held too much power over my adult self-image.

There are still times when I see the imagined remnants of my eighth-grade face staring back at me in mirrors. Like a parent, I coddle the child and tell him that his awkwardness is not a permanent condition. When I look at the picture now, I see a boy who knows what he looks like but doesn't understand that he will grow out of it. He will, eventually. He's not so bad-looking after all.

MOTHER NATURAL
Bente Engelstoft

It's natural for kids to become fixated on a subject: dinosaurs, stuffed animals, trains, space. My fixation was a little different. Growing up, I had a bit of an obsession with boobs. What they looked like, what they felt like, could I have some, when I would get them . . . Can I get a timeline, please?

My mother is Mexican and grew up in a rather strict Catholic household, but my father is Danish—a people so liberal that the government provides free, no-strings-attached healthcare and everyone is okay with that. A people so liberal that every student over the age of eighteen is given free money to study. A people so liberal that, until recently, I don't think they even sold the top half of bikinis. And so I was never taught to be ashamed of my body. In fact, I was known as the streaker around my suburban Houston neighborhood because of my refusal to wear swimsuits at the pool.

My point being, I knew my parts. And the parts I was most interested in were my boobs.

Now, my mother was rather stacked. A petite woman of five-foot-one, she rocked a gorgeous pair of C-cups, and I knew that one day I would carry the same with pride. But then I noticed that there were pictures of my mother from before she had me and in them something was noticeably missing. *Where are the boobs, Ma?*

I was very disappointed to learn that it took pregnancy for my mother to grow a pair.

So I turned to my father's side. Three brothers, no women save for my grandmother, whose breasts I had seen many times on visits to the beach in her small seaside town of Hornbaek. Farmor did not believe in sitting in wet swimsuits after a dip, so she would change into a dry suit, loud and proud in front of the whole beach. I remember noticing that her nipples were longer than my mother's. I assumed that was because she had had three children while my mother had only had one. My Mexican grandmother gave birth to thirteen children, so I could only imagine what her nipples must have looked like.

Once, when I was about five or six, I saw an ad on the back of a Danish design magazine my mother loved to look at, *Bo Bedre*, "Live Better." The ad was for a perfume, and the image was a naked red-headed woman covered in flowers everywhere except for her nipples. Her *pink* nipples. My mind exploded. Just when I thought I had seen it all, there was a pair of nips in my favorite color. Who knew that they came in more than one shade? Why hadn't anyone told me? It was a serious breakthrough in my breast-related research. Now, I knew anything was possible.

Around this time, my girlfriends started wearing training bras. They were basically cropped camisoles with floral patterns and matching underwear. I wanted one. I can't remember whether I asked my mother for one and she said no, or if I imagined she would say no, so I never asked. But I definitely didn't have one. One day while my mother was folding laundry, she came across a pair of my dad's worn briefs that had a small hole. She knew my father would never throw them away, so she ripped the hole even bigger so that they would be unwearable and set them aside to be thrown away. Being the weirdo only child that I was, I began to play with the broken underwear. I found that the rip had created a hole in the crotch large enough for a head, and the leg holes were the right size for arms, and well, I'll be damned if the elastic waist wasn't just the perfect size to turn these torn briefs into my first training bra!

I would wear my bra around my room, admiring the false maturity I felt it gave me. I plotted how to get more underwear, but before I could get that far, my vanity got the best of me. I was so proud of my DIY bra that I completely forgot the means by which I had acquired it, and so one day I just went into the kitchen and said, "Mommy, I have a bra." I lifted my shirt to reveal my father's raggedy, faded green briefs.

My mother looked at me. Her face was confused, trying to understand what she was looking at, and then suddenly she started laughing. Harder and harder. "Is that Daddy's underwear?"

I was mortified. I was trying to show my mother the woman I had become, and she was just standing there, bracing herself against the counter with tears forming in her eyes. Once she finally collected herself, my mother sat me down and told me that one day I would get breasts, and even if it didn't look like she had much "pecho" before she was pregnant, she did in fact have boobs as a teenager. And then she told me something I will never forget: "Whenever your boobs itch, it's because they are growing." She meant it as a small and encouraging tip, but to me it felt like the final clue.

And so after that, anytime I felt a slight itch, I scratched my chest with pride, knowing that I was growing some boobs.

OTHER PEOPLE
Erin Claxton

While I was home a couple weeks ago, I looked through old pictures. I got to a stack from my early high school days and said to my mom, "I wish I would have realized how cute or, at least, not unattractive I was while in high school." She replied, "You were very attractive; you just let what other people thought get to you." This surprised me.

I always felt like I had done a good job of being my own person. Wearing my men's jorts along with my orange-and-blue glitter turtle shirt with pride. I was never told I wasn't pretty. Never bullied. I had no reason to think I was anything other than a beautiful girl. Perhaps because I reached puberty before everyone else. Like. Way before. Resulting in weight gain and more hormones than a fourth grader can comprehend. I felt like The Hulk in a classroom full of children.

I was the tallest girl in my grade for many years. In fact, I remember once in fifth grade, Mrs. Gardiner's class, we were talking about runway models and how they're all very tall. Mrs. Gardiner looked right at me and said, "You know, Erin could be the only one of us who could potentially be a model." Obviously, I turned bright red and knew that couldn't be true, 'cause I wasn't pretty enough or skinny enough to be a model. I mean, duh. That had to be what everyone else was thinking, too. It wasn't that I thought I would much rather be a lawyer or actor or in the WNBA (an honest-to-God past dream of mine) instead of a fashion model, but that I wasn't pretty enough.

Why? Was it society? The magazines? Was it because I was the only girl out of my friends who hadn't had a boyfriend? It certainly wasn't my home life. My mom constantly told me how pretty I was, and my family was always very proud and loving. What made my little-girl brain react like this?

This belief followed me through the years. Assured me that I was doing fine in life in every way except my appearance. I wasn't depressed. I didn't let this tiny voice rule my life, but it was always there. Guess what? Let's be honest—it's still there. It will always be there. Now, I'm just better at shutting it up.

So, even though I had a solid chunk of years with purple, wire-rimmed glasses, unruly curly hair that usually resembled a mushroom cap, and a fashion sense that attempted to combine sporty and cute and failed—I think my personal awkward phase is the one inside my head. The one that was still around after I discovered hair product and started shopping for bras outside the sportswear department. The one that trapped me inside of that uncomfortable, confused, newly pubescent girl even though I was far beyond her.

If I could go back, I would write that girl anonymous notes celebrating parts of her that were beautiful and unique and perfect just for her. Imagine how uplifted she would feel knowing that a stranger took the time to tell her she's beautiful. I mean, imagine how all of us would feel.

On the train today I saw a little girl reading a book called *A Smart Girl's Guide to Liking Herself*. Although it's sad that a book like that even has to be written, I'd love to thank whoever wrote it, whoever published it, whoever bought it for that child. This little gem has got a head start in self-esteem building. I think we could all take a page straight out of that book.

STOP BEING POLITE AND START GETTING
REAL WORLD

Niki Madison

Hi, MTV! I'm Niki. I'm sixteen. I'm from Edwardsville, Illinois. You should pick me for *Real World* because . . . because . . ."

Many evenings of my high school career are spent preparing my *Real World* audition tape. However, I never audition. I don't think I'm interesting enough because everyone selected for *Real World* is some sort of social anomaly who was not only adopted by disabled, interracial, agoraphobic, and alcoholic parents, but they are all also drop. Dead. Gorgeous. And I'm embarrassed that my true obsession with the MTV show is the relationships—a few of the cast members of *Real World* always fall in love. Like season one's Eric Nies and Julie, Hawaii's Colin and Amaya, or Boston's Jason and Timber (who wasn't a cast member, but still . . .). I want to be Keith Sweat "Twisted" over somebody.

I'm a sophomore in high school in the year of our Lord TRL. I'm in Mr. Minicello's Romantic Poets English class. The assignment we're given requires us to write a Valentine's Day poem about someone or something that we love and admire. Each day in class, I sit and stare at him: Jordan Harper. His alabaster skin sparkles with more of a luminous glow than any tween vampire novel can describe. His ginger hair, flecked with gold, falling in the most perfect of symmetrical, middle-parted bowl cuts, shames Backstreet Boy Nick Carter's hair. He is beautiful.

I decide to confess my desire. I write and rewrite my poem until I feel I have captured the longing to be the strings he strums on his guitar, which typically rests against his teal blue locker. I note how his flannel American Eagle button-down and baggy Abercrombie & Fitch carpenter jeans look perfectly styled with his Doc Martens. I carefully confess my admission of many dreams of kissing what I imagine to be the softest of lips. Clocked in the safety/delusion of a sound track of Billie Myers's "Kiss the Rain," Seal's "Kiss from a Rose," Jessica Simpson's "I Wanna Love You Forever," and Jennifer Paige's "Crush," I construct my masterpiece.

On the day the assignment is due, I am filled with nerves as, one by one, we go around the classroom and read our works. Sarah writes about her love for cheerleading. Bobby writes about the joy of scoring a game-winning goal. Girl after girl writes about our teacher, Mr. Minicello, who is young and athletic, but no Jordan Harper. Finally, after everyone else has taken their turn, dressed in my Good Charlotte T-shirt, new boot-cut jeans, and distressed vintage-style green cardigan (RIP Kurt Cobain. I'm still reppin' you, boo), I read my poem aloud.

There are giggles and snickers. There are eye rolls and awkward grins. As I finish my poem, I stare down at the desk, humiliated by the deafening silence. Why isn't Jordan, despite my three-hundred-pound frame, carrying me off like Baby in the *Dirty Dancing* lift? Why aren't we engaged in an intense make-out session? After all, that's how Cher and Josh (from *Clueless*, duh), and of course the greatest teen "almost couple" Angela Chase and Jordan Catalano, show their affection?!?

Days later, I learn that Jordan is dating my close friend, Megan Kurtz. Five-foot-six, size-four, DD-bra, Megan Kurtz. Of course. Despite that intense high school emotional clusterfuck, to this day,

I get instantaneous crushes, and I love hard. I'm no longer ashamed of that. Now I don't need the *Real World*, because I'm living it. This six-foot-one, plus-sized, queer black woman with several college degrees who grew up in the heart of white suburbia *is* interesting enough. I see beauty in people—inside and out. One day, I will find a pop culture—loving nerd who will see the awesomeness in me. Someday, someone will walk up to me and say, "Let's stop being polite and start getting real."

Chapter 5

Celebs 4ever

TO LYNDSAY, THANKS FOR THE GREAT STORY! LOVE, REBA

Lyndsay Legel

When I was a child, I didn't just *love* country music; I was collect-country-music-trading-cards, record-every-country-music-awards-show (both on VHS and cassette), write-weekly-letters-to-country-stars in love with country music.

From the get-go, my parents had a microphone in my hands, and they had me performing Randy Travis's "Diggin' Up Bones" and George Strait's "All My Ex's Live in Texas" in our living room. We have VHS tapes of me at age four, singing these songs with the conviction and bitterness of a middle-aged divorcee. While I didn't understand the content of the negligees and ex-wives songs, I understood the rhythm. I understood a story was being told. And I was in love with those stories.

By the time I got to fourth grade, I had narrowed my sights and focused my passion into one singer in particular: Reba McEntire. I spent my days in rural Iowa listening to her songs on my Walkman while mowing our twenty acres of lawn. Above the sound of the mower, I'd belt the lyrics to "Fancy" and "That's the Night That the Lights Went out in Georgia." I read about her in my *Country Weekly* magazines (which were tenderly cared for and alphabetized on my bedroom bookshelf). I read her autobiography. I prudently studied her biographies. At one point, I could have told you every . . . single

... detail about her life. Husband's name? Narvel. Birthdate? March 28, 1955. Middle name? Nell.

With my handwriting skills excelling by fourth grade, my letter-writing efforts to Reba ensued. I would even go so far as to make my mother take pictures of me holding my father's guitar, which I did not know how to play. I sent these pictures to Reba so she could see that I had what it took to be a star just like her. How many letters I sent her, I don't know. What I told her in these letters, I can't remember. But I wrote and wrote with hopes that she would, just once, write me back and acknowledge my love for her and invite me to visit her in Nashville.

The summer after fourth grade, my parents helped me realize this dream. On a blistering August day, they packed me up in our burgundy Cutlass Sierra and drove me to see Reba McEntire in concert at the Iowa State Fair. I was confident I was going to meet her. Why wouldn't I? I was clearly her biggest fan. In preparation for our meeting, I packed my yellow backpack with the following items: my Reba music video VHS tape, my Reba books, my Reba cassettes, my Reba CALENDAR, my Reba T-shirts, and, of course, a Sharpie so that she could sign every last piece of my Reba memorabilia. After the show, I stood around with my ever-so-patient parents and waited for her to emerge and meet me. She never came.

I remember that walk back to the car like it was yesterday. My head was hung low and tears bit at my eyes as I trudged my backpack full of unsigned Reba McEntire merchandise to the trunk. While I was so thankful to have seen her singing in the flesh, my nine-year-old heart was broken. I had been so close to her, yet I was still so, so far.

That next fall, when I entered fifth grade, my parents open-enrolled me into a bigger school where I would have the opportunity to learn how to type on a computer and meet more friends. Not knowing a soul at this new school, which was five times the size of my previous school, I knew I had to dress to impress. I carefully selected my outfit for that first day: my hot-pink, cutoff shorts and my XL Reba McEntire T-shirt. Being the new kid in town, I quickly acquired the nickname Reba. Now, at age twenty-nine, I for the first time consider the possibility that people may have been calling me that out of jest. But fifth-grade Lyndsay responded to that nickname with absolute honor.

By sixth grade, I had expanded my hobbies to also include story writing. My stories were all basically the same and included a plot that focused around Reba and a starstruck girl who hung out with Reba all the time. One particular story I wrote called "The Ninth Caller" was about a girl (me) who won a radio contest. The grand prize was a trip to Nashville to spend a weekend with Reba and her backup singer, Linda Davis. Using the typing skills I had acquired through my new school, I typed up the story (including a title page) and sent it to Reba. I sent one to Linda Davis, too, just for good measure.

Weeks went by, and I had almost dismissed "The Ninth Caller" from my memory, when I hopped into my mom's car after school one day and she handed me a big manila envelope. The return address label pierced my heart with excitement. It was an envelope from Re—ba— *McEntire*. I tore open the envelope (the whole time reveling in the fact that she had touched the same envelope that I was now touching and that her spit had possibly sealed the envelope that was now MINE).

Inside, I found an 8-by-10 glossy that read, in Reba's pen, "To Lyndsay, Thanks for the great story! Love, Reba." I could barely breathe.

I tore out of the car and ran into the school to show my teacher, Mrs. Soeder, who had also taken to calling me Reba. I ran through the halls showing anyone who would look. Tears of joy flooded my eyes. My hands shook. Reba knew I existed! She read my story. We were FRIENDS.

I proudly framed and hung my 8-by-10 glossy on my bedroom wall, and I continued to love Reba throughout the years. But, as all things often do, my love for her faded. Junior high brought me exposure to bands like Spice Girls and Ace of Base. I retired my Reba T-shirt to adorn more "trendy" duds like JNCO jeans and No Fear T-shirts. But even though my obsession for her eventually faded, I will never undermine the fact that, for most of my childhood, I was able to pour my energies into admiring a strong, confident female who tastefully shared her gift of music with the world. And while Reba McEntire most definitely does not know who Lyndsay Legel is, Lyndsay Legel is most definitely a better person because Reba let me love her and shower her with letters and look up to her in a way I have never looked up to anyone else in my life.

MINNIE MOUSE, MY HERO NO LONGER*
Claire Linic

Minnie Mouse is the spokesperson of domestic goddesses everywhere. Minnie Mouse keeps her house cute all the time. Minnie Mouse's relationship with Mickey inspired my dreams of love. Minnie Mouse's polka-dotted dress summed up all that I hoped the future held for me.

When I was six, and my parents told me that we were going to Disneyland, I felt sure that this was my moment to bloom. Growing up, I was hopelessly odd: I preferred to be called Chest; a turkey that police named Rambo attacked me; I permed my bowl cut. Disneyland was my chance to meet my idol, who I knew would make me feel cool.

I envisioned the future in which I would tell the kids at school about my trip, and the stories of my adventure would take me from "Claire? Isn't that the girl who collects human teeth?" to "Claire? Oh, yeah, she's that cool girl who went to Disneyland."

I brought my autograph book. I met Goofy, Chip 'n' Dale, and two different versions of Mickey. Briefly, I became addicted to meeting these characters. How lucky that we all lived in the same place and they so casually walked around to greet me! I couldn't imagine life any differently. After riding Peter Pan's Flight three times, though, I'd still yet to meet my main girl Minnie.

Soon, that would change.

---

* Originally published in *The Hairpin*

*

In retrospect, Disneyland was the last time I believed I had a shot at a perfect life. If only I'd known then how many meals I would eat in bed, or the number of times I would yell, "I'm walking away now, not because I'm dramatic, but because I have nothing left to say to you," or the percentage of those times that would occur on first dates. Or, that after a final fight in a toxic relationship, I would take nothing from his apartment but two steaks out of the freezer and a Bruce Springsteen album—all I needed for a fresh start.

At the Disneyland point in my youth, I still saw Minnie's squeaky perfection as a real possibility, and the Mme. Mouse herself as just the person to tell me how to achieve it.

On the last day of my Disney trip, I finally saw her. My hero. My friend.

Between the churro stand and bushes shaped like Disney characters, Minnie appeared before my eyes. My world filled with magic. I broke away from my parents and ran toward her. If my hair had been longer than my bowl cut, it would have blown in the wind. Instead, my hair just sat right on top of my head, like always, and Minnie didn't seem to care. My new best friend threw her hands up in the air to hug me. While still running, I stretched out my arms to mimic her greeting.

Then, it happened.

With those beautiful white gloves, Minnie clutched at her neck. I halted. Vomit started to trickle out of a slit I'd never noticed before. My role model took off her head. Minnie projectile vomited.

Men came out from what seemed like nowhere—an area that has since become clear to me as those weird underground Disney tunnels. One of the men promptly took Minnie away from me. The other man picked up the head with her smiling face and eyes pointed right at me. He lingered for a moment.

"Minnie's not feeling that well right now," he said.

My parents caught up to me and tried to explain everything. It was too late. All this had happened in about five seconds. Magic didn't necessarily die for me that day, but it did get violently ill and then decapitate itself.

What died that day was the foundation of my domestic-goddess self-imagination. If Minnie could take off her head and vomit, then what would stop me from eventually going on a date with a man who preferred to be called "$bill"?

Nothing, apparently.

*

It's been twenty years since Disneyland. Now, I'm married to a wonderfully weird man, and my house is never clean, and I still would be over the moon if the nickname Chest finally caught on for me.

I told my husband this story on our first date. He reciprocated with his own stories of childhood trauma, and we laughed, and it was awkward magic.

I can only hope that Vomit Minnie and her Mickey equivalent have been able to do the same.

BACKSTREET BOYS CHAT ROOMS

Sara Grossman

When I was twelve or thirteen, my best friend was OBSESSED with the Backstreet Boys—especially Nick Carter. And she spent a lot of time in a Backstreet Boys chat room. I was into chat rooms because . . . well . . . ASL? So I just hung out there with her and her other BSB-obsessed friends.

I stayed in touch with one of them over the years, and we both ended up moving to New York City. When we hung out, we would never tell anybody how we became friends since she is from Virginia and I grew up in Florida and our paths never crossed before New York.

Fast-forward to a year ago when I was visiting the city after moving to Denver. I had a smattering of my friends around the table at Dallas BBQ, and we're all drinking frozen drinks the size of our heads. After a few drinks, I grab Cat and tell everybody that I need to make an announcement:

"CAT AND I MET IN A BACKSTREET BOYS CHAT ROOM WHEN WE WERE TWELVE. NOW YOU KNOW."

She was a little mortified, I think. But it was also incredibly hilarious. And now it's one of my favorite party stories.

SLIMMONS

Shaun Sperling

Growing up, one of my favorite places was the Richard Simmons's workout studio. Tucked away in a strip mall in a suburb of Chicago between a Chinese restaurant and a 31-Flavors, it was aptly called Slimmons. My mom would take me with her after work, but I didn't join the other kids in the play area. I'd sit in the back and watch the women flap their arms in the air from side to side as they sweated to the oldies. I memorized the routines, so  sometimes when the music moved me, I'd join in the fun. After class, we'd pick up Chinese takeout and a pint of Rocky Road for dinner.

One evening, during a routine to "It's My Party," I had to use the bathroom. On the bathroom wall was a large poster of Richard Simmons dressed in his iconic red striped shorts and rhinestone-studded tank top. As a twelve-year-old, I loved and hated Richard

Simmons at the same time. I appreciated him for his flamboyant exuberance, but I was also embarrassed by it.

I sat down on the toilet and grabbed a *Muscle and Fitness* on top of the stack. I thumbed through the pages and looked at pictures of scantily clad, bronzed men and women. When I reached the centerfold, I was paralyzed. On the left side of the page was a woman in a gold bikini flexing her biceps (meh!). On the right, a man stood in a royal blue speedo and held a barbell over his head. Without so much as a glance, my eyes raced over the picture of the woman. My gaze landed on the center of the right page—directly on the royal blue package.

I felt a spark, a tingle, a jump. It caught me off guard, and I quickly looked up. My eyes landed on Richard's. He glared at me like he knew my dirty little secret. I shifted back to the magazine, first to the left side, at the woman. I felt *nothing*. I then looked back to the right, at the man, and I felt *something*.

No, I thought, *this can't be right*.

I repeated the steps several times—Richard, Woman, Man—Richard, Woman, Man. I don't know why, but it was *that* moment, as I took a dump at Slimmons, while Richard glared at me, that confirmed what I had been trying to suppress for years:

Yep, I was definitely gay.

A STAR TREK BABY
Eli Mandel

One of my first memories is watching the series finale of *Star Trek: The Next Generation* when I was five. That was the year my family moved to Bellingham, Washington, for some reason before promptly moving back to Central California. It was also the same year I attended my first *Star Trek* convention. It was in Vancouver, British Columbia, and I don't remember much from it. But I do remember being excited that people there seemed to like *Star Trek* as much as I did.

This convention also brought me one of my first memories of embarrassment and shame. There was a sort of simulation at the convention in which a commander on a big screen would give you orders. You were sitting at an Ops station (LIKE DATA!), and you had to carry out the orders. I was sitting on my aunt's lap, trying to do it, but my adorable little fingers were too small and weak to push the buttons, so I decided to walk in front of the screen and ponder things just like Captain Picard. As soon as I got up there, though, a nerd yelled at me. I was mortified. The only consolation I got was taking a picture with a cardboard cutout of Geordi La Forge.

I remained a big *Star Trek* fan, but wasn't a full-fledged Trekkie until high school. Junior year, I bought all seven seasons of *Star Trek: The Next Generation* on cheap Chinese DVDs. I watched the whole thing, and it completely changed my life. When I was a child, Geordi had been my favorite character. (I like to think that's unrelated to *Reading Rainbow*, but you don't have to take MY word for it.) But in my Trekaissance, Data was a clear stand-out. He strived to be something more than the sum of his parts, even though it was physically impossible. Though he wanted nothing more than to be a part of it, Data looked at humanity and was confused by what he saw. That really spoke to my nerdy little self. I subsequently bought and watched all of *Voyager*, *Deep Space Nine*, and the original series.

Let's jump forward a bit to the summer before my senior year of college. I was living in a house with my buddy, Loren, in Santa Cruz, California. I made him watch *TNG* with me every

night while we drank High Life. Loren's grandmother lived in Santa Fe, New Mexico, as did my girlfriend at the time, so we took a little road trip out there to visit. Along the way, we stopped in Las Vegas for the world's largest *Star Trek* convention. I was beyond excited, as I hadn't been to one since I was five. I was most excited to get my picture taken with Brent Spiner, who played Data.

I think it was fifty bucks, and I shelled it out without a thought. As I was in line to take the picture, the very attractive Vulcan female in front of me turned and told me how nervous she was to meet him. She was shaking. "Don't worry," I said. "He's going to be so nice and this is going to be the best moment of our lives!" She seemed moderately encouraged and shook less. As she reached the front of the line, Brent greeted her with a big smile.

"Hi!" he said with an enormously jovial smile. "How are you? I'm Brent, what's your name?"

"I'm Rebecca. I'm so nervous," she replied. "I can't believe I'm meeting you."

"Oh, don't be nervous. It's very nice to meet you, Rebecca. Hey, let's look at the camera and have a great photo. One, two, three. Cheeeese! Now that wasn't so bad, was it? So nice to meet you, Rebecca."

He gave her a big hug and sent her on her way.

Oh, hell yeah. This was going to be the greatest moment of my life. If he was that nice to Rebecca, *imagine* how nice he would be to me! I approached Brent Spiner, the man who portrayed my favorite fictional character of all time, a person who, although I had never met before this moment, influenced me more than any teacher or coach ever could.

"Hi, Mr. Spiner!" I said.

"Hey, how's it goin'?" he replied as he casually threw his arm around my shoulder. The photo was taken and I was on my way. There was no grand greeting or jovial hug. He didn't really notice me at all! Though he was my idol, I was nothing to him.

That thought hurt for a bit. But really, *why would he care*? I'm just one of millions of nerds. That's the beauty of *Star Trek*; it means so much to so many people. It changed my life, and it's changed millions of other lives, too. I am so grateful that my friends know me as the *Star Trek* guy, and whenever I meet another *Star Trek* person, I can talk to them about it. The series has an optimistic, humanistic view of our future, and it's something I'll be proud to be a part of for the rest of my life.

BEANIE BABIES SPREAD THROUGH MY CLASS LIKE A DISEASE

Wes Perry

Beanie Babies spread through my fourth-grade class like a disease. They simply started appearing on students' desks, and every day the collections grew and grew.

The moment I saw them, I knew I had to have one, so one day after school I begged my mother to drive her sky blue '93 Toyota Previa straight to Toys "R" Us. I ran to the stuffed animal department and picked out a small brown dog with big, sad eyes. I named him Droopy.

At school the next morning, Droopy was all the rage. I was the first boy to have a Beanie on my desk, and all the girls were passing him around, saying how cute he was.

But one girl was *not* having it. Michelle was the queen of Beanies, and before the year was over, she would become the reason for the official "one Beanie per desk" school rule after her desk became so cluttered she could hardly do her work.

Michelle knew her stuff; she was serious about the pocket-sized plush.

Right before recess, she stopped by my desk, parting the flock of girls who'd gathered to gawk at Droopy. "Can I see it?" she asked. As I handed him over, her face looked like she'd asked for diamonds but was given coal. She inspected him briefly, then said, "This isn't a real Beanie Baby. He doesn't even have any tags."

He was an impostor. A fake. A plush pretender. You can't even buy Beanie Babies at Toys "R" Us I soon learned; they were only sold at a small boutique a few stores down called Rubber Duckies. As the years went on, I got to know Rubber Duckies very well, but first things first.

That night, I took Droopy into my bedroom and closed the door. "There's something I need to tell you," I gently said. "You're not a real Beanie Baby. And that doesn't mean I love you any less."

But we both knew that wasn't true. Soon my collection grew: first was Legs the Frog, followed by Garcia the Bear and Happy the Hippo. As my Beanie family grew and grew, Droopy got pushed farther and farther away from the bed and into the closet.

I haven't looked into my childhood closet in years, so I wonder if he's still there, waiting for me in the dark. Knowing my parents, though, he was probably donated to charity long ago.

So where is Droopy now? I'd like to imagine he's with a new family, one that's never even heard of Beanie Babies, who couldn't care less about his "brand." In my mind, it's a place where a droopy dog with no tags is free to simply be.

Ed's note: Adult Wes still loves his beanie babies, because they (Wes and beanies) are always awesome. Feel free to make this pic the desktop image on your work computer.

Marching Bangs

I used to cut my own bangs. They had to be perfectly even. Sometimes I got them right on the first try. The day before band picture day, it took a FEW tries. While they are casually swept to the side, I assure you, every wispy strand of bang is exactly 0.78 inches long.

—Laura Bloechl

Chapter 6
After-School Activities (excluding Detention)

FOOTBALL JOCK TURNED THEATER KID
Robert Bacon

Does this look like the kid you hated in high school? That idiot on the football team who drove a Mitsubishi Eclipse and constantly quoted *Tommy Boy*? Yeah, unfortunately I was that guy, but you would be surprised to find out that I was also a theater nerd. I even remember the day I became one.

Freshmen English class was just about over. Mr. See, our teacher, would always give us the last five minutes of class to work on our assignments, but I took that as "Bacon-gets-attention time." I was being my typical self, doing stupid bits and making horrible jokes, when Mr. See called me up to his desk. The whole class made an *ooooooooooooohhhhhhh* sound because they knew I was in trouble. As I was walking to his desk, the bell rang, and everyone poured out of the classroom. I really liked Mr. See, and I wanted him to like me, so I was nervous about what he was going to say to me in this now empty room. Mr. See looked up from the book he was reading and said, "Bacon, have you ever heard of the forensics team?"

Turns out that not only did my school have a forensics team, but we were the best in the state. Oshkosh West was notorious for not only winning the weekly competitions at various schools, but also winning the state competition every year. We were back-to-back-to-back state champions, and it was mostly because of the drama teacher, Mr. Lynch. Mr. Lynch was an amazing man who knew how to get the most out of his students, and he really cared about everyone he worked with. That was a lot of work, considering the team was so big we would have to take two buses to competitions.

I was in one of the most competitive categories: solo humorous. You perform eight minutes of a play, with multiple characters, by yourself. You simply change your voice and physicality to show a new character. There were some seriously talented kids in this category, and if you wanted to win, it took a lot of work. I would practice multiple times a week with our forensics coaches after school and by myself. I would save the score sheets from the three judges every week and read over them constantly, trying not to make the same mistakes again.

I can honestly say Mr. See, Mr. Lynch, and the other coaches taught me it takes more than just being funny to succeed in comedy. I owe so much of everything I do to them.

FAKE GLASSES AND SHARP NOTES
Tyler Gillespie

Hey, Band Kid!

I know how much you hated the clarinet and I know you didn't need glasses, even though you wear a pair in this school band photo. I get you're a bit insecure right now, but I'm still going to start with the bad news before the good (the way you'll want to receive information even as an adult).

Bad news: You still don't wear glasses—well, sometimes to read, but the jury is still out on if they're necessary.

You remember sitting in the chair and looking through a tiny eyehole at the other side of the room. You could see the horse you were supposed to identify, but you called it a squirrel. If it was a dog, you called it a cat. To prepare for this test, you had spent at least an hour reading in the dark—something you had heard strained your eyes. All the hard work needed results.

When you're an adult, your grandmother will say the eye doctor didn't have the heart to tell you that you passed the eye test. She will remember the doctor saying something like, "If his eyesight was as bad as he pretended, then glasses wouldn't have been able to help him at all." Your uncle, the ophthalmologist, gave you a pair of non-prescription tortoise-shell glasses so you'd feel better. You thought glasses made you look smart and would help you blend in at school. You may not have needed the glasses, but they sure were sharp.

More bad news: You never climbed the ranks of the band geeks like you secretly wanted. Those band kids were too musically inclined to include you in their shenanigans. You were pretty good at the violin, an instrument your grandparents took you to lessons for so you'd get your hands just right. But you gave it up because it wasn't cool (this was an uninformed opinion). They didn't have a violin section in your school's band, so you justified the switch to woodwind.

You might have been able to make second chair—but probably never first because those kids were really good—if you would have played something other than the clarinet. Spoiler alert: You never learn how to use a reed properly. Your uncle bought you the clarinet, and it was too expensive to just give up.

I'm not sure if this is economically sound advice, but it's something to hold on to: If you can rent something you're unsure of—like you could with the clarinet—do it. Don't buy unless you know your investment will pay off. Also, if you want to play the French horn, your original choice, do not under any circumstances settle for the clarinet.

Now for the good news: I want to tell you that you were really, really bad at the clarinet. Like, seriously. The thing is, though, it's okay to be bad at things (and sometimes preferable). You are a rigid and by-the-book Capricorn—a sign known for perfectionism. This Capricorn-life translates into you not wanting to look stupid if you fail. Try not to care as much. I want to encourage you to be bad at as many things as possible.

That last piece of advice might sound all wrong, but what I'm trying to say is *I want you to put yourself out there*. If you only do things you're good at, my friend, you won't be doing much. (I'm in no way knocking you, just saying there is so much out there to do and your skill set is . . . specialized.)

Open yourself up to experiencing stuff you wouldn't think you'd like. Contrary to what you think, you don't have to be good at something to have fun doing it.

Please, don't let me forget this about fun—you need to have more of it.

Truthfully, you have more fun doing stuff you aren't great at—like singing and telling jokes—because you feel less pressure to do them well. Without pressure to be the best, or to even be considered good, you are free of a lot of the self-consciousness that held you back as a teenager.

Be bad, and laugh at yourself. It's so much more fun than feeling like you have to be perfect all the time. Plus, this whole fun thing I've been telling you about will help you with the stuff you are actually good at doing.

Hindsight can be 20/20, even when looking through a pair of fake glasses. Now, turn off the band room lights and get ready for your mall-kid stage.

Oh, I almost forgot a little more good news: You were way ahead of your time wearing nonprescription glasses. Fake glasses will be a trend that pops up nearly fifteen years after this picture was taken. People refer to these visionaries as *hipsters*. If anyone asks, just say it'll be an accepted look in the future.

OK, ONE FROM DETENTION
Suzy Exposito

"Ashes to ashes / dust to digust," I scrawled in my journal, "I collect all their lectures / burn them too, I must!"

(I'm pretty sure I wrote this in detention.)

—Suzy X

IT WAS THE PLOT OF EVERY AFTER-SCHOOL SPECIAL COME TO LIFE

Stephen McDonald

When I was a kid I used to cry . . . a lot. When I lost games, when anyone was mean to me, when I felt even the slightest bit scared—I was a crier. I was the youngest of three boys and my two older brothers were twins, so I got very used to losing every fight we ever got in. I was not a wimpy-kid crier, but a kid with hair-trigger tear ducts and a moral compass that let me know I was doing something wrong and triggered waterfalls to fill my face. This trait made me an awesome liar (as long as by *awesome* you mean that when I went to lie to my mother, I would burst into tears because I felt sick to my stomach). Crying never seemed to be too much of a problem—kids cry sometimes—until I hit middle school. When a third grader cries, it's reasonably normal, but when you are in seventh grade, you become that kid: the one who cries.

Now, I was never very good at paying attention.

My whole life, I have had my head firmly placed among the clouds, which has sometimes left me behind my peers in social interaction. In seventh grade, I experienced a succinct moment of understanding that I had missed a turn into young adulthood. I was sleeping at a friend's house with one other boy. It was fun. He had a pool and one of those electric plasma ball things where electric air would run to your hand when you touched the glass. It was summer and we were young. So, as the young are prone to do in semi-rural Ohio, we commenced in a bike ride through dirt roads of a still-being-built suburban community. We rode our bikes to a small natural pond in the center of the new community. Everything was normal. I had been to this pond before and had a great time, but little did I know that while my head was in the clouds, things on the ground had changed.

Before I knew what was going on, one of my two friends was bending a pop can into a makeshift pipe and the other was pulling out a plastic bag of weed. It was the plot of every after-school special come to life, but the primary thing that was not communicated in those specials was that, when the peer pressure moment came, I would have a brain filled with enough adrenaline to cause my hands to shake. My voice cracked. To them, we were all young adults who ventured into the world to do adult things and have adult experiences. To me, we were kids. That's how I wanted it to stay. So, I did what I knew how to do: I cried. I cried a lot. Like snot bubbles and dry heaves kind of panic crying. Seventh-grade me was not in the wrong. He did what he knew how to do. But later I found out this story was told to others and my tears were the punch line.

Years later, I still get a small, sick feeling in my stomach over that day, but it did cement something in me: crying is something I do. I am not afraid of it. I don't do it as often as I used to, but when I feel my eyes well up and droplets cascade over my cheeks, I don't care that I'm a twenty-six-year-old man. I welcome those tears like a long-forgotten friend. We hang out and catch up. Neither of us is angry and we both understand that, as time has gone on, we can't hang out as much as we used to. But I always know that when I am in trouble, my tears and I can meet up on my pillowcase and by morning everything will probably feel a bit better.

NAIVETÉ HAS ITS PERKS . . . AND SO DOES BEING AN "UPPIE"

Shaun Sperling

On a Friday in late May 1997, I walked into seventh-period choir ready to rehearse for my final choir concert. The room was large and bright with three levels of risers surrounding a grand piano on a square carpeted platform. But instead of our choir director, Ms. Neutson, perched at the piano, there were four starry-eyed twenty-somethings dressed in bright, primary-colored clothing. They stood side by side and smiled like a Hands Across America greeting card.

I was a senior in high school and ready to graduate in just three weeks. At my school, it was a given that you would go on to college. Of course, there was the random deviant who got pregnant or overdosed on designer drugs, but the college-going rate was about 99 percent. As a nice Jewish boy with an incessant need for attention and affirmation, I was ready to be part of the 99 percent.

The group introduced themselves as the international sensation, Up with People. I had never heard of Up with People, but I was immediately captivated by their radiant energy, impeccable white teeth, and perfect posture. There was a girl dressed in a kimono from Japan, a blond-haired-blue-eyed boy with a sexy lisp dressed in overalls from Nebraska, a young man dressed in a poly-cotton robe with an African pattern from Ghana, and a woman with a seductive accent.

After their brief introduction, they sang and danced to a song called "Everybody's Everybody." The lyrics went:

Everybody's everybody and nobody is the same.

Everybody's everybody and it doesn't matter where you came from.

I found the song very profound. They went on to describe the Up with People experience: a one-year program in which young people between the ages of eighteen and

twenty-seven from all over the world travel to multiple continents to perform a musical about diversity and multiculturalism. During the year, *uppies*—that's what they called themselves—stayed with host families, moving from city to city every three to five days and doing community service projects. They played a promotional video of boys dancing and singing, exotic-looking girls holding babies, and groups of people of different creeds, colors, and religions holding hands harmoniously.

This group's visit was dual-purpose: first, to sell tickets to what they described as an international spectacular for the senses. And second, to tell us how we, too, could participate in this once-in-a-lifetime opportunity.

My best friend, Erick, was slouched in the seat next to me mocking the group. He leaned over and said, "I'd rather get a root canal than sit through that."

I didn't react, but I didn't have to for him to know how I felt.

"Oh no, you're not buying into this shit, are you?"

"No, I'm just, no . . . I, I'm just listening to what they have to say. It's interesting . . . what they're doing."

"Oh please, don't drink the Kool-Aid."

I was enticed by everything Up with People had to offer—international travel and the opportunity to change the world through song and dance. But there was something else . . . *the boys*. Although masked like normal boys, I saw through the propaganda. It was as if they were calling out to me—young gay men beckoning me to join them, to join them on their homosexual love parade around the world. I was an impressionable, gay eighteen-year-old with a flair for the dramatics and a desire for sophistication—they had me. Hook, line, and sinker!

I had been the first person to ever come out of the closet at Stevenson High School. My first two years of high school, I had been tormented by the school bully, Wally Stiltz, and every popular kid who followed him. At the time, I avoided most social interactions and self-expression at all cost. But one afternoon during sophomore year, I had had enough. I was walking down the long hallway that stretched across the length of the school as Wally came around the corner. I braced myself. Per usual, as I passed him, he said, "Hey . . . you're a faggot." Instead of my normal response, which was to ignore the insults, I stopped and turned around slowly. I walked toward Wally and looked him dead in the eye and said, "Yeah, I *am* a faggot."

Wally quickly turned around and got the hell out of there. Word spread fast, and I was prepared for the backlash. But as I walked the halls with my head held high past groups of cheerleaders, jocks, and stoners, the layers of fear and shame started to drift away. So did the bullies. Wally never bothered me again, and I started making friends. I gained a certain amount of popularity myself, or maybe infamy is more like it. I fought against opposition from the school board and faculty to form the first support group for gay and lesbian students in a Midwestern high school.

I was proud to stand for what I believed in and proud to be a sort of figurehead for being the gay kid. But still, as a senior, I felt like I didn't have a place where I belonged, so I went to the Up with People show that night. It began with young people—many, many, many, many of them homosexual—storming the aisles waving scarves in the air and encouraging people to get on their feet and dance. I was transported to exotic locations, moved by the music, and energized in a way only live theater could do. The show ended with a rousing rendition of their signature theme song, and I joined the cast by swinging my arms and clapping from side to side:

Up, Up with People, you meet 'em wherever you go.
Up, Up with People, they're the best kind of folks you know . . .

After the show, I raced down the theater steps to the woman in charge. "Hi, Catherine," I said with just the right amount of Up with People enthusiasm. "My name is Shaun, and I have a deep desire to change the world through song and dance." Catherine gave me a knowing grin and escorted me to a lunch table outside of the theater. She called over the all-American, lispy boy from the choir class.

Yes, I thought, *he's soooo dreamy.*

"Shaun," Catherine said, "this is Todd." Todd reached out his hand and said hello. I took Todd's hand in mine and looked deep into his big, blue eyes. I was silent, but I thought to myself, *Oh Todd, please rescue me and take me far away from here.*

We sat down, and they took turns asking me questions.

"Do you have experience performing?" Todd asked.

I was paralyzed, so he prodded, "Do you sing or dance or act?"

"Yes!" I said. I *must* have told him about my involvement in school plays and community theater, but I don't remember. He asked some follow-up questions, and then I must have been drugged by the colors and the energy of Up with People, because I heard him beg me to run away with him.

Join me, Todd beckoned, *join Up with People so that we could sing and dance together, and make out on top of the Eiffel Tower, cuddle on a gondola in Venice, and make love on a deserted island in Tahiti.*

"Yes, yes, yes," I responded.

When I got home, my mom was on the couch watching television, and I began my sales pitch immediately.

"How was your night?" she asked.

"Mom, oh my God, the most incredible thing happened today."

"What, what is it, sit down and tell me everything."

"Have you ever heard of Up with People?" I asked.

"Oh sure, the Christian group that sings and dances around the world."

"No," I snapped. "That's a common misconception. Up with People is not religiously affiliated."

I went on to tell her about the show and regurgitate everything I had learned from the presentation earlier that day. Up with People was not a hard sell for my mom. She was always convinced that I would be famous one day. So it made perfect sense to *her* that I would be discovered in Up with People.

The following Monday, Catherine waited for me outside of choir class to tell me the good news. Despite the rigorous vetting process and without an audition, resume, or personal statement, I was accepted with a scholarship. Soon, I would be jet-setting in luxury planes, performing on world-renowned stages for dignitaries, politicians, and celebrities. With Todd by my side. I couldn't wait to tell everyone the news. I expected my friends to be wild with jealousy. But, at best, they were skeptical. Erick pleaded with me not to do it. Others called me naive and stupid. Some laughed in my face.

When I told Mrs. Jacobs, the head of the drama department whom I had spent four years seeking validation from, she scoffed, "You're not serious, are you? Up with People? You know it's a cult, right?"

A cult . . . no it is not a cult, I thought. *Fuck them. They're just jealous.*

I arrived at Up with People's Denver headquarters in July 1997. I got off the bus and looked around at hundreds of happy young adults from all over the world. They were ready to make a difference. I wore a necklace with rainbow rings, popular in the 1990s to not so subtly identify one's sexual orientation . . . like I needed that. I didn't. I didn't hold back my flamboyant exuberance. To everyone I met, I gave a hug and said, "Hi, I'm Shaun from Chicago." And I was met with the same overly enthusiastic introductions. Everyone was eager to make an impression. That afternoon, I spotted Todd from across the field. My heart raced, but I approached him as casually as possible.

"Hey, it's Todd, right? Remember me, Shaun from Chicago?"

"Of course I remember you," he responded. I went in for a hug, as he put out his hand, and we ended up in a half-hug with our hands caught between us. We stood there uncomfortably for what felt like an eternity, until he said, "So . . . you made it." He told

me what an incredible year it was going to be, and then after one of many silences, he said, "Nice necklace."

"Oh, thanks, this old thing?"

"What does it mean?" he asked.

I hesitated. Surely he knew what it meant. Maybe he was testing me, so I humored him. "Well, it means I'm gay."

"What?" He was stunned. "Gay, gay—like, you like dudes . . . gay?"

"Uhhh, yeah."

"Oh," he responded abruptly. "Well, I'm sure I will see you soon." And then he dashed off.

I was used to that kind of reaction, but I wasn't expecting it *here* and from *him*. Very quickly I realized that being gay, or I should say being *openly* gay, was not part of the Up with People paradigm of diversity. That year, I sang and danced in flamboyant costumes through fifteen countries: on hay bales in Arizona, on the steps of a castle in Germany, and in town squares throughout Europe. I stayed with more than sixty families: on a Mormon compound in Utah, a convent in Finland, a trailer home in North Carolina, and an army camp in Portugal. I met hundreds of people and listened to their complex, beautiful, and sometimes tragic stories. I learned more about myself with each one.

The friends I made that year remain some of the closest and intimate relationships that I have today. Every five years, we get together for the official Up with People reunion, and we jump right back into it, like the naive and adventurous kids we were. At the last reunion, Todd was there *with his husband*. At one point, he thanked me for being brave enough to be myself back then. I had no idea that I made that impression on him.

I set out that year to find a place where I belonged. I discovered that we all have our own stories—the belonging is in finding people to share them with. I guess being naive really has its perks . . . and so does being an *uppie*.

DELUSIONS OF GRANDEUR
Cathie English

I was the fat kid. At five-foot-two (I eventually topped out at five-foot-four-and-three-quarters) and one-hundred-something pounds, I wasn't the fastest kid on the block. Fat, yes; fast, no. But I had four older siblings and three of them were athletes. And if you remember anything from eighth grade, it's the year your teachers and coaches want you to try every available activity to determine your talents. Well, my brothers were all very good track athletes. It was in our genes!

My coaches determined that since my oldest brother was a great hurdler (he was six-foot-one and long-legged), I could probably hurdle, too. So, they convinced me to run the low hurdles. Event #1.

Even though I was short and "chubby," they thought I had a bit of speed. Or, being from a very small school (a hundred students), I doubt they had any Babe Didriksons available. (I read everything about her—this was before Jackie Joyner-Kersee, of course.) So, they wanted me to run in the 4 x 440 relay. (Yes, it used to be called this—each person ran 110 yards.) Little did they know I had no coordination; it took several weeks to practice the handoff. I ran the slow leg. Event #2.

My third oldest brother was an excellent long jumper. I was not. How do you get a big butt up in the air enough to get height and distance? Answer: You don't. Event #3.

My final event, #4, was the event that no one, absolutely no one, wanted to run: the 440-yard dash. It's the gut-buster race. You can't jog it; you're expected to go full out.

Back in 1974, in a small school, the eighth graders had one track meet. We ran on an asphalt road out to the local cemetery to get into shape. The road was marked with distance increments, and I would groan after I had gone only about half a mile. But I persisted, and the day finally came for me to run and jump!

My long jump was unmemorable except that I threw out my lower back. In the 4 x 440 relay, once I handed off the baton (barely), I face-slammed the track. That was back when it was a cinder track. You wipe out and it's gonna hurt. In the low hurdles, I fell into the last hurdle but picked myself up and finished. I have a three-inch-long scar above my right elbow. To end the day, I gutted out the 440-yard dash, the race nobody else wanted to run. Thankfully. It meant I got a white fourth-place ribbon.

Although I had hoped to be a Babe Didrikson, to hear the shouts of the crowd and relish a medal around my neck, my sole year of track shattered my delusions permanently. My track career ended with the reality that I would never grow out of my awkward phase. I have the scars to prove it.

BORING RAP STAR
Alan Linic

Having finally figured out what I wanted to do with my life, I was supposed feel successful. Instead, this turned my senior year of college at James Madison into a slow and strange waiting period. I had an obligation to earn my degree before I could set out on my own to do what made me happy.

In the meantime, I went through the motions. I took dull classes like Intro to Ocean Geography to round out my degree requirements. I picked up and dropped hobbies constantly to make the time go by. I logged more than three hundred hours of *Left 4 Dead* 2 and spent an embarrassing amount of money on Magic: The Gathering cards.

My grades slumped under the weight of laziness and apathy. I felt myself dying creatively, and as a result spent a lot of time in class thinking of creative ways to die. I wasn't depressed or angry or even particularly lonely—just uncomfortable and bored. To be fair, I doodled just as much about riding bears and puppies doing handstands. I wrote some okay raps and awful poetry.

I shambled around campus, convinced I was the only one who knew exactly what he wanted to do and where he wanted to be while not doing anything related to it in my academic career. This feeling lasted until I graduated. One month after that, I was finally empowered enough to pack my entire life into a backpack and a duffel bag and board a train to Chicago to try my hand at improv.

Since the day I arrived, I've been doing comedy in the city I love best—and the same drive and self-knowledge that made me feel unfocused and out of place at my college make me feel purposed and happy here.

Like some kind of success.

FOLLOW THE LEADER
Erin Hickey

I'm not entirely sure how I got into musical theater. Maybe it was genetic—maybe it was my parents' incessant playing of *Miss Saigon*—but I was hooked at a young age. It was all Disney movies all the time. I used to dress up as Mary Poppins and sing "The Perfect Nanny" to my preschool class every morning. So imagine how excited I got when I found out the Northbrook Community Theater group was doing the live-action musical version of *Peter Pan*. At six years old, I was perfect to play a Lost Boy, or if I got lucky, Nana the Dog!

My mom saw the audition notice and brought it to my attention. It was a chance for her to get me out of the house and a chance for me to be the diva I knew I could be. I watched the movie over and over for research. Peter was great, but man, those Lost Boys were killing it! I could do that, no big!

One of the songs that the Lost Boys sing in Walt Disney's classic version is "Follow the Leader." It's perfect for a budding six-year-old diva; it showed off what little vocal range I had. My grandma had a grand piano and a Disney songbook. I cracked that bad boy open, found "Follow the Leader," and began to practice the song. By the end of the week, my thirty-two bars of that song were great. No other six-year-old could best me.

Cut to the audition day. I'm in my nicest dress, my platinum bangs are plastered to my forehead, and I'm holding my Disney songbook. I was ready.

"We'll see numbers one through ten; please follow me into the audition room," the auditioner called.

I was confused. I was pretty sure I would be going in alone, but now I'd have to watch eight other children do their best Lost Boy impression before I would get a chance to strut my stuff. Whatever. I was ready.

We all walked into the room and sat down in metal folding chairs against the walls. The director introduced herself and advised us to stand in the middle of the room and sing the song. The first child stood. She had no book. What an amateur! She announced she would sing "Tender Shepherd." The pianist began to play.

At that moment, I wasn't confused about why the pianist knew the song; actually, I was impressed that he could just play it from the title. I did start getting confused when the second auditionee stood up and announced he too was singing "Tender Shepherd." By the time the third sang "Tender Shepherd" like an angel, I was starting to feel sick. There was no way everyone just found that song on their own. It's not even in the movie!

I had to watch five more kids stand up and sing "Tender Shepherd," and I started freaking out. I should just start learning it now! I could do that. "Tender shepherd, tender shepherd, help me count your . . . passing sheep?" Well, that doesn't make any sense. Why are the sheep passing? I couldn't do it. I felt nervous and panicky; my hands got so sweaty I dropped my Disney songbook. I hastily picked it up and scurried over to the piano.

"What are you singing today, sweetie?" the very nice pianist asked the trembling six-year-old.

"Um, 'Follow the Leader'?"

"Okay, well I don't know that one, but I'll try."

A few minutes ago, this pianist was magical. Now, the magical pianist suddenly can't read sheet music? Unacceptable. I walked to the center of the room and wiped my hands on my dress. I looked up at the director. The music started.

And I started crying. I couldn't do it. I couldn't be the only one singing a different song! I ran out of the room as fast as my legs could carry me. I burst through the doors and into my mom's arms. I wept for days and vowed never to ever audition for anything ever again.

Much like many of my adult vows to stop drinking after a long night out, that didn't stick. I kept going on auditions. And while there were some devastations along the way (not getting cast in *The King and I* was a big one for this little redhead), I never stopped trying. I just kept plugging along, kept practicing and memorizing. And even if it's just in my car, I've never stopped trying to be the diva six-year-old me believed I could be.

I also learned eventually that most community theaters have an audition workshop for children that teaches them which song to sing . . . which explains that whole phenomenon of every eight-year-old in the North Shore area knowing "Tender Shepherd."

Now I can join them since I now know "Tender Shepherd" by heart. My six-year-old self would be so proud.

Chapter 7
Summertime Stories

WHEN NATURE STRIKES
Irene Marquette

When I was in elementary school, my parents sent me to day camp for a few weeks every summer. It was fun. I liked it. I made friends, picked up new skills, saw neat things, and drank orange juice out of little plastic tubs with foil tops. But I wanted more. And I wasn't afraid to beg for it.

Finally, the summer after sixth grade, my parents sent me to Rancho del Chaparral Girl Scout Camp in New Mexico. A couple girls from my troop were going as well, and I was over the moon anticipating what summer had in store for us. Friendships, secrets, archery, horseback riding, mess halls, a little harmless adventure. Maybe my breasts would grow. I'd get my period if I was lucky. I'd have God's-eyes a'plenty to hand out to my family when they came to collect me at the end. Oh, I couldn't wait to be the hero of my very own summer camp movie.

But I made my first misstep the very first night around the campfire. We were learning great songs like "One Tin Soldier" and "Barges." I had my little campfire song booklet I bought at the general store and was furiously flipping through it trying to keep up. These girls were so much older, cooler, and wiser than me! Finally, I found my time to shine when they said they'd be singing "Desperado." GREAT, I thought, surely they will want a performance of this classic! I stood and launched into a soulful rendition of the Eagles song only to open my eyes and see everyone laughing at me.

"I don't know what you're singing, but that's *not* 'Desperado,'" they said as they snapped their gum and tossed their hair. And then they sang their version. "What a big tall man, was this Desperado / from Cripple Creek way out in Colorado! And he horsed around just like a big tornado / And everywhere he went, he gave a WOO HOO." I couldn't hate them! They were so sophisticated, miming galloping on a horse and then spinning like a tor-nah-do. I swallowed my pride and got on board.

This was the first of a series of small humiliations I experienced while I was there. Some of them were the result of teasing from the other girls and some of them I brought upon myself. Like my decision to mimic an infomercial and vacuum-pack all my clothes in freezer bags before I arrived. And my desire to wear only a giant polka-dot shirt and black polka-dot leggings every day. The worst offense of all was that I decided early on that I wasn't going to poop for the entire week.

Maybe it was a fear of doing it in a place away from my home (at this point in my life, I was a bit neurotic about "doing it" at school or other foreign places), or it came from not wanting the other girls to SMELL IT, or maybe it's that slightly dehumanizing way we fantasize about our own lives as though we are characters in someone else's work. Young camping ladies in movies do not excuse themselves to drop a turd. So, I didn't. I just refused. I held it in day after day without much trouble until about Wednesday, when I changed my mind and realized that I *couldn't* "do it." I had willed myself into extreme constipation.

That night, I stayed awake imagining the damage I had done to my body. Surely, I was irrevocably poisoned by my own filth. My bunkmates would find me in the morning and from that day forward I would forever be the girl who died from choosing not to poop. I didn't want to be that kind of ghost! My stomach started to hurt. Before breakfast, I went and tried. Oh, how I tried. Nothing came out, and I started to panic. I ran to my best friend and told her what I had done (checking "secrets" off the old camp to-do list!), or not done, as it were. She was appalled, confused, and went to get our counselor, who was probably seventeen and cared not for a neurotic prepubescent non-pooper. What a summer SHE must have been having.

It wasn't long before everyone knew. There was an outright summit between my counselor, the nurse, and the girls in my cabin convening just outside the latrine. Why did she do it? What is wrong with her? YOU OKAY IN THERE? And the whole time I'm just trying to squeeze this entire situation away. The nurse gave me some anti-constipation medicine and had me go lie down in my cabin until things "worked themselves out." I was supposed to gently massage my stomach and roll my legs up to help get "things moving." When I was absent from group activities that afternoon, everyone knew why.

I wish I could say that was the last time I had to learn the lesson that the things you actively try to ignore have a habit of rearing up and making you deal with them. These days, I try to face my problems head-on and don't care so much about where I am when nature strikes.

HOW I SPENT MY SUMMER VACATION: CIVIL WAR REENACTMENTS

Erin Lann

I don't know what kind of family vacations my parents envisioned for us when my brothers and I were infants, but I can't imagine it was Civil War reenactments. Or "living history" trips to Williamsburg. Or figuring out how to get historically accurate rifle replicas on a plane.

My older brother, Matthew, was a Civil War fanatic. As a reenactor, he proudly represented Ohio's Fifth Volunteer Infantry, and for most of his early teenage years, dragged us to every major Civil War battlefield in the United States.

My parents, ever supportive, would gladly pack the car every summer, and we would hit the road for a few weeks of nineteenth-century misadventures. There were two main reasons why I loved these vacations: One, we always stayed at a Howard Johnson, and I could steal dozens of chocolate muffins from their continental breakfast. Two, we ended our trip on the East Coast, at a museum or memorial dedicated to the Revolutionary War.

At seven, I was *obsessed* with Thomas Jefferson. I was captivated by tales of his inventions, foreign diplomacy, and his presidency. I kept a copy of the Declaration of Independence on my closet door, right next to my Jonathan Taylor Thomas poster. I can't begin to measure the amount of pent-up sexual frustrations that those boys caused me in my early years.

My affinity toward Jefferson, and all things Colonial, manifested itself in a variety of adorably uncomfortable ways. I boycotted tea. I always wore my hair in an eighteenth-century ponytail. I got a Felicity doll—and if you don't know what that is, you're dead to me. I had a Colonial parchment-and-quill set that I would use to leave cryptic notes around the house for my family. I watched *The Patriot* on repeat. I wrote pre-Internet Thomas Jefferson fan fiction. I once tried to salt meats for the winter. I also tried to churn apples into apple butter, and I made a men's Colonial-era shirt to wear as a nightgown. As you can imagine, I was the envy of every reenactor.

In the summer of 1997, we were planning our annual pilgrimage to Gettysburg. It's a huge event—kind of like a Civil War Coachella.

After Gettysburg, we would drive to Virginia to spend three days at Colonial Williamsburg and Monticello. And after weeks of pleading, my mom consented to construct a Colonial dress for me to wear. After all, Matthew had head-to-toe Union regalia, so there was no reason I shouldn't have an overly elaborate frock of my own.

For the next month, my mom rose with the sun every morning to fashion my gown (she was a two-time 4-H clothing construction state finalist, *no big deal*). I slowly worked myself into a hyperactive ball of excitement that no amount of sleep aids could contain.

For days leading up to our trip, I couldn't eat. I had the singular focus of a stag in heat. Colonial Williamsburg. Monticello. I was going to the Motherland. Nothing was bringing me down.

Not even four days of record-breaking Gettysburg heat could tame my excitement. I impatiently watched seas of navy and gray reenactors run around battlefields, my thoughts always creeping back to the beautiful, maroon, custom Colonial gown in our minivan.

At the end of day four, we loaded our suitcases into our minivan's rooftop carrier, drove to a Ramada just outside Williamsburg, and unpacked the carrier in the parking lot. I took out my dress and starting playing with it in the parking lot. I showed several other reenactor families that also unloaded for the night. "Leave the dress up there," Mom instructed, as she put it back into the garment bag and stashed it away. "I don't even want to chance leaving it in the hotel." We locked it in the carrier—safe and sound.

The next morning, I leaped from bed at a healthy 6 a.m., already shaking with adrenaline. I got dressed, stopped at the hotel buffet to stuff my backpack with chocolate muffins, and went to the car with Mom to get my dress.

Before I reveal what happened next, I want you to know that, unbeknownst to me, I was enjoying my last few moments of childhood innocence. I can safely say it's been a steady downhill fall from there on out.

The rooftop carrier was open; the lock had been cut off and the latch was damaged. Fearing the worst, Mom climbed up and looked inside. Empty. The only thing left in the carrier was the white doily-looking thing I was going to wear on my head.

I would quickly like to point out a few facts: First, this dress was clearly homemade, and as such, of no real monetary value. Second, this burglar had to open the garment bag that held my dress, rifle through its contents, make the educated decision to discard the white doily-thing, and take the rest of the bag. Third, the lock on the carrier was really thick, which means that the person who robbed me had the strength of a grown *fucking* man. And finally, this dress was clearly fitted for a chubby little girl, which begs the question, *What are you doing with it, grown fucking man????*

Another reenactor had clearly seen me fiddling with the dress the night before, bided his time in the parking lot, cased our joint, found the necessary pliers to break into our carrier, and taken the dress back to his lair where, I like to imagine, he still pulls a Buffalo Bill with it several nights of the week.

As the realization sunk in, I collapsed in a sobbing puddle. Stunned and panicked, Mom demanded the hotel try to uncover the thief from security camera footage. The hotel employees were of no help. I wailed, a mixture of tears and muffin burps. I was victim to a seemingly random act of violence, committed by one of our own.

Reenactors stick together; we're the nerds whom not even other nerds can deal with. At the end of the day, we only have each other— and this was blatant betrayal. My heart was broken; my faith in the community shaken. I told Dad that I hated reenactors and never wanted to see another reenactment ever again.

By the time we arrived at Williamsburg, my face was stained red with tears, my throat was dry from crying, and the glaring sun made me sick. I sat on the stoop of the Governor's Palace and hung my head in shame.

About this time, a woman who was dressed for the period approached me and asked what was wrong. I explained what had happened, choking back tears. She stood thinking for a moment, then smiled and asked Mom and me to follow her.

She led us into an alleyway behind a row of Colonial homes and took us into a dark shop. When she turned on the lights, I saw that we were in a showroom filled to the brim with Colonial dresses.

"I manage the dress shop in the historic district," the woman explained. Her name was Debbie; an older, robust woman who had perhaps spent too many hours alone with her cats. Like most reenactors, she was a total weirdo, but genuine and kind. As Mom regaled our story, she shook her head in disbelief. She, too, knew the treason that had been committed. She turned to me and said, "Normally we're closed today, but these are special circumstances. I've only got one dress for little girls, but you can have it."

The dress, to be fair, was an ill-fitting white bag suited for a homeless man's baptism. It was a far cry from my dress. But, it was something—if nothing else, a vote of confidence in the reenacting community that I desperately needed. Debbie outfitted me with primrose-pink accessories as Mom and I thanked her graciously. To this day, I think of her from time to time and smile. I hope she retired to a beach town somewhere, where she's regularly asked to dress up as George Washington and give speeches or something.

My love for Jefferson and reenacting has yet to fade; I still spend parts of every summer on the East Coast, learning about the Founding Fathers, visiting their homes, and stealing chocolate muffins. I just booby-trap our carrier.

A TEEN WITH BABY TEETH

Kelley Greene

Let me start by saying that, growing up, I was both a late bloomer and an overachiever. When I was in first grade, my classroom had a special tooth-shaped poster board on the wall where the teacher would place a photo of you after you lost a tooth. I was an excellent student, so I had my photo up on the special board for kids with good grades. Naturally, I believed that I should be on *every* board there

was to be on. But my teeth just weren't getting loose. I remember complaining to my mom that it was unfair that kids were getting recognized for something I had no control over. There was no way for me to get on that damn board no matter how hard I tried, which I found infuriating. I prayed for the day that I'd find my first loose tooth so I could get noticed for it.

I never did get on that board, though, because I didn't lose my first tooth until I was in third grade. By then, there were no more tooth boards on which to be recognized. Losing teeth was pretty well normal at that point, and the majority of my classmates already had a good number of permanent teeth. But I didn't care. Nothing could put a damper on my high when I lost that first tooth. I was catching up! Plus, I was finally gonna rake in some of that sweet Tooth Fairy cash that my friends had been rolling in for the past two years.

Around the time I lost my second tooth, our family dentist had recommended I see an orthodontist since I was going to need braces. The orthodontist decided that my teeth were moving too slowly and that they needed to pull all four of my top front teeth to "make room" (what is this, a dinner party?) for the two adult front teeth to come in as straight as possible. That was just the first stage—I'd have four more bottom teeth pulled later that year.

I can't believe I was actually excited to get my teeth pulled, but I damn well was. I mean, I was scared that it might hurt, but still . . . *Hell. Yes.* Eight teeth out in one year. I mean, that was practically all of them, right? And you think a dollar from the Tooth Fairy is good? Who *knows* what she gives when you have more than one tooth at a time to offer her!

As prescribed, I went in and had the teeth pulled. It was a painful nightmare—not to mention, I got blood on my favorite dinosaur sweatshirt. (As an aside, the T. Fairy did give me a full twenty bucks as a consolation. Also, teeth are mega gross when they still have the roots on them.) *At least,* I thought, *I'll have my new teeth soon and this will all be over.* Four teeth down. I was moving up in the world.

However . . . those fancy new teeth that I thought would come right in? Well, they didn't. For *months,* I had no front teeth at all. This means no eating apples, carrots, anything you have to bite into, unless it's cut up first. It also means getting professional soccer photographs taken when you only have half a smile. My most vivid memory of this tooth-less time in my life is visiting Six Flags Over Texas that summer. I was ecstatic. After riding the Runaway Mine Train for about the fiftieth time, my cousin and I grabbed some ice creams from a nearby ice cream stand to cool down. I got a push-up pop since I knew it was soft. I chomped down on it, taking the best "bite" I could, when something sharp stabbed me in the gums. Turns out that there was a tiny plastic Rumpelstiltskin man hidden inside the pop. *Surprise!* Gums bleeding, I bawled to my mom, who stormed back over to the ice cream stand.

The thing I remember most is watching my mom ask the teenager running the stand, "Why would someone do this to a child?!" And now, I think, the answer is probably because they thought the little surprise inside the push-up pop would be fun for kids. You know, kids with teeth.

Even through all that, I remained enthusiastic about losing teeth. I never gave up on reaching the same development stage as my peers. I had the remaining four pulled by the dentist later that year and, of course, finally started to get some permanent teeth in. I lost more on my own and things finally started looking up.

I lost my last tooth in tenth grade during homeroom. My friends and I were sitting around talking and eating Now & Laters when I felt my loose tooth finally come out. "*YESSS!* My tooth fell out!" I exclaimed to a room full of fifteen-year-olds. I ran to the bathroom, pulled it out, and tossed it (and the Now & Later) into the garbage can. (Because I was fifteen. Tooth Fairy? Puh-lease.) When I got back to the room, I noticed everyone was staring.

"It's okay, it wasn't, like, a real tooth, it was just a baby tooth," I assured everyone.

"You still have *baby* teeth?!"

I'd always longed to be recognized for losing my teeth, but that wasn't quite what I had in mind. Luckily the bell rang and I was able to escape any further questions. Shortly thereafter, I was finally able to get my braces. I had them put on September 10, 2001. If you're wondering how I remember, it's because I was in the school's office turning in my absence excuse notice from the orthodontist when I found out about the planes hitting the World Trade Center. Yes, that's "where I was." Seriously.

I had to wear braces all through the remainder of high school, and I didn't get them taken off until after I'd graduated. This means that, for ten years, no one I grew up with ever saw the straight teeth I'd waited my whole life to get. But you can bet your ass I wore my retainer every damn day between the time I got them off and my ten-year reunion. And I still do.

So, I guess, my Awkward Phase still has some remnants. But they make me who I am, and I'm totally okay with that. And so are my teeth.

DAY-GLO ROLLERBLADE CHAMP
Tyler Gillespie

*D*an Jansen Better Watch Out! I wrote the above on my second-grade "Top Banana" poster—a project every student did to showcase the multifaceted aspects of their lives. Dan Jansen (of course I don't need to tell you this but I still will) was an Olympic gold medalist for speed skating in 1994. A quick Wikipedia search tells me that in 1994, "after a career full of setbacks," he won a gold medal in world-record time. I've always identified with the underdogs. His Wikipedia

page also shows me his photo, a photo that can only be described as "all-American looking." While I am super happy for Dan's success and jawline, he was just one of my many gold-medal friends.

For the summer Olympics in 1996, I made a giant poster board with an updated medal count—gold, silver, and bronze—for each country, which took forever because I had to crayon-color in a million white circle stickers. During the track and field finals, my grandmother and I each wore one gold shoe (of her pair) to be like Michael Johnson. And, please, if you ever meet me, do not get me started on the women's gymnastics "Magnificent Seven"—especially Dominique Dawes or my feelings on *you-can-do-it* Kerri Strug.

In the above "Top Banana" picture, I told Dan Jansen to "watch out," but speed skating wasn't what I was usually doing when I closed my eyes and rollerbladed down my grandparents' street. I grew up in Florida, and our only ice-skating rink was about half an hour away at Countryside Mall. My real rollerblading friends and competitors were figure skaters: Michelle Kwan, Oksana Baiul, and Surya Bonaly (the French skater who did backflips on the ice!).

When I snapped on the buckles of my rollerblades, I'd often imagine that I'd be competing in the Olympic figure-skating final. My routine music was always Tina Turner's "Rolling on the River" because I was roller (get it?) blading and thought the judges would approve of my creative music tie-in.

With Tina blasting in my mind, I'd roll on down the street, past Dan Jansen and Michelle Kwan. No one could stop me or my triple lutz, triple toe loop combination. Okay, well, the mailbox did stop me once; I had my eyes closed and skated into it.

Summers of childhood imagination and scraped knees taught me how to pick myself up and the adult me is Olympic-thankful for that.

MY DAMN NOVELS
Brooke Allen

Each summer my brother and I would leave the cozy bottom half of a duplex in Milwaukee that we shared with our actress mother to stay with our dad and his shiny new family in the suburbs. More specifically, we went to visit the pool. Strutting around in a swimsuit all summer would have been a dream come true for many preteen girls, but at the time, I was around ten years old, and all I wanted was to take art classes, eat chocolate bars, and read my damn novels.

Now, my brother not only could adapt and have a blast anywhere you stuck him, but also could instantly become the most popular kid in the room. He was one of those shockingly cute kids. I remember mom's friends saying, "That boy. He's going to be such a heart-breaker! And Brookie, she sure loves to read!"

During those summers, we would be dropped off each morning at 7 a.m. for swim team practice at Le Country Club. Swim team was so deeply unimportant to me. We used to travel to other country clubs for meets, and I remember once getting in trouble for reading and eating french fries in the snack shack instead of competing in the back-stroke. At another meet, I managed to compete instead of eat, but I backstroked my head straight into a wall, then stood up to the horri-fied faces of the crowd and said, "Did I win?" . . . and then I blacked out. So you can see how fantastic this whole experience was for me.

Each day after swim practice, my lean, tan, and outgoing brother would go off with his cool, tan friends. I, on the other hand, a drown-ing Brontë sister, would then be subjected to the ultimate humil-iation: synchronized swimming. Imagine, if you will, the meanest, richest, prettiest girls from your junior high school. Now, imagine them gracefully popping in and out of the deep-deep end in high-cut swimsuits. Imagine a whole row of them in perfect unison swirl-ing and twirling in the water with names like Tiffany and Kimmy and Susie . . . and at the end of the row a chubby little ten-year-old named ME . . . who needs to wear a noseclip and a sun hat and just wants a goddamned cheeseburger. It was brutal.

At the end of each summer, the synchronized swim team shellacked our hair into buns and bought matching scrunchies and sarongs to perform a water show for our parents. Yeah, we did. I was even allowed to choreograph one of the land-dances one year—that's the dance you do before jumping in the water (it's a synchro thing, you wouldn't get it). I choreographed a very special dance to "She Drives Me Crazy" by the Fine Young Cannibals that resembled something between the Macarena, the Vogue, and sit-ups. As far as my history of being a choreographer goes, it was one of my proudest moments. Although I wasn't asked to choreograph anything the following year . . . or ever again.

The next year, the show was going to be even bigger. I was super excited until the coaches decided we needed boys in the recital and so, of course, my big bro was the first to jump on board. I decided to use his perfect "sinking ballet leg" and "dolphin turns" to my advantage and nabbed him for a duet. At least the focus would be off me, and I would be the envy of all the Kimmys for dancing with the hottest tween boy at the country club. My brother. This whole situation was more than my dad could handle. Between my inability to dance and my brother's being involved at all, I'm amazed my dad even showed up to this monstrosity.

So there we were, much to my father's horror, land-dancing awkwardly to "Do You Love Me?" (It was the *Dirty Dancing*–themed synchro show, HOT.) My brother jumped in the water as I nervously untied the heart-patterned sarong around my waist. (This is real, you guys. . . . We all had little cloth sarongs that we obviously couldn't swim in so at the last minute we stripped them off. I remember even as a kid thinking, *This seems wrong*, which I guess is better than thinking, *I've found my calling!*) I plugged my nose and jumped in after him. "I'm gonna drown you!" he whispered. And he tried . . . he certainly tried.

＊

Author with brother. Eds. Note: He really is cool, look at his skateboarding skillz!

After swim team and synchro practice each day, it was time for my favorite event: lunch. We were allowed to order a certain amount of food daily from the snack shack at the club and put it on my dad's bill; the account number was 602. Now, I can't remember what I wore yesterday, but by God I remember the code for the snack shop at the country club. I always ordered all my food for the day at one time and ate alone at a picnic table. Since I ate this all at once, I would be ravenous by dinnertime, which was around the same time my dad got off work and took some time to relax and unwind . . . at the country club. I lived there. And when you live somewhere, you have to make it your own, you know? Instead of working on my tan and learning how to french braid my own hair with the other girls, I built a fort out of lawn chairs, laid my towel across it, and crawled inside to read *Gone with the Wind* or *Death of a Salesman* or something else equally as inappropriate. I rarely swam unless I was forced to, perpetually terrified that I would start my first period in the middle of the pool and force everyone to run screaming in a *Jaws*-like fashion to the nearest exit. I was not going to be that girl. So, I hid in my fort and read. I was THAT girl instead.

Oh, and the moms at the country club! They all had these helmets of hair and long tan legs and giant hair bows that coordinated with their swimsuits. They read catalogs and wore too much makeup, and I hated them passionately. Mostly because I missed my mom so much. Plus, these women were like *Real Housewives of Suburban Wisconsin*. They gossiped about the children, and I overheard them from inside my fort. "Jenny So-and-So is getting kind of horsey-looking" and "Donny So-and-So got grounded last week, did you hear?" and "Brooke Allen, is that her name? She is so . . . creative." (For these women, *creative* had the same pitiful connotation as "Poor thing, she was just born that way.") While I sometimes resented that my mom wasn't a cookie-baking-PTA-going-girl-scout-leading kind of mom, I never desired that she be anything like these ladies whom I found vile. I ached for my mom.

I have an entire landscape of memories involving her. There was the time she woke us up late one night and took us down to the lake to see a particularly beautiful full moon, or the time she dropped me off at college and drove away shouting, "I love you! Always use a condom and don't ever drink blush wine—it's trashy!" Or there was the time in high school when I went through a rough patch and lamented, "I thought my mother was supposed to be my guardian angel, so why is

my life so shitty?" and she replied, "Oh, honey, she IS your guardian angel, she's probably just a little drunk right now, though." But the truth is that whenever I think about her, I remember the following image most vividly:

I was lying on a country club lawn chair, burned to a crisp, reading *Les Miserables* or *Anna Karenina* perhaps, when all of a sudden I heard, "Hi, chickie." I looked in front of me and saw dirty sandals, knobby pale knees, cutoff denim shorts, a Paul Simon "Rhythm of the Saints" T-shirt, and that fluffy wild red hair. She was like this glorious abomination among the other women at the club. What, to a Kimmy or a Tiffany or a Susie, might be a masterpiece in humiliation was to me an angel.

"Mom?"

"Jesus Christ, you look like a lobster. Come on, let's go."

I don't remember where we went or what we did, just that my mom heard me somehow, crying out for her from this world of manufactured beauty, and had come to save my ass. We spent the day together away from the club, and I talked while she listened, which was the only thing I needed. By 5 p.m. she dropped me off, and I tearfully shuffled back to my lawn chair, as though it were just a dream. "I love you, Angel-Face. Don't mention to your dad that I was here, okay?"

It wasn't until years later that I considered the magnitude of what she had done. Defied custody regulations, marched brazenly into the check-in area of the country club where, mind you, she was a former member (it's not written in the bylaws, or maybe it is, but you know, no ex-wives allowed), and waltzed right past those sorority-sister-summer-job front desk girls, through the ladies dressing area (a.k.a. the Hall of Second Wives), and out into the pool area to find me.

"Mom? You're here?"

That is motherhood. That is sacrifice. To listen for the heartache of your pudgy-clumsy-melancholy-sunburnt kid and save her from even one more day of humiliation, that is true love.

Looking up at her from my lawn chair that day, I didn't speak for a moment. I knew even then that this image of her was the one I would have burned into my head forever, the one I still to this day see first when I think of her, even though she's older now and the fire has gone out of her hair a bit. It's the image that comes to mind whenever I hear the word *mom*.

Or whenever I hear a Paul Simon album.

I AM NOT ALONE
Michael Hinder

I always thought my awkward years would be in high school with the whole awkward teenager thing. My entire friend group started dating and a few of them started having sex. You know how much of a big deal that was back then. I always wanted someone to date, but didn't really know what I would do from there. Sex was never really a goal for me. But I wanted to fit in, so I forced myself to try to think the way they did. But at the end of the day, I was still the same person.

College made socializing worse. My friends seemed to be fitting right in, and I felt more alone than ever. But even more than that, I felt like I didn't know myself. Classic college woes, *I know*. I saw a counselor and talked to my parents and eventually things started to turn around. I made some friends and became better friends with the ones I already had. But I still felt like something was missing. Things like how guys on my floor would be so excited to go out partying to hook up with strangers. It's all they would talk about, and I just didn't see the appeal. But it wasn't just the appeal in real life. I'd watch shows like *Mad Men* and *Game of Thrones* and not understand why sex was a rampant part of the show. It seemed like it ruled over some of the characters (both real and fictional), and I just couldn't relate. I wasn't a teenager anymore, so what was going on?

Fast-forward to my first year of graduate school. By this point, I figure it's just the way I am, and there's no explaining it. But I'm a math guy; I always want answers to things I don't know. And one day my answer came. While talking about these issues with a friend, she asked if I was asexual. Asexual? I had no idea what that meant, so I looked it up. Asexual means that you aren't sexually attracted to people or have little to no interest in having sex. It was me. It described me better than anything I had ever read.

And it answered so many questions! It was literally just who I am, but now I knew! I never thought that just a word, a label, could make me feel so much better about who I was. There was a community of people out there who were the same as me. Statistically, I'll never meet them, but it doesn't matter. I am not alone.

I am not alone.

I need to say it again. I am not alone!

It's too easy to fall into the trap of trying to fit in and just be "one of the guys." Whenever that happens, I just feel like I'm acting and not being myself. There's nothing wrong with me. I'm going to not understand things and there's nothing wrong with that. Despite what my worries say, there are a lot of nice people out there who won't think less of me for not being like them. There's nothing to be afraid of. It's time I stop saying it and start believing it.

My name is Michael, and I am an asexual man.

Chapter 8

Awkward-Kid Redemption

GRIM LOOKS, HANDS IN COATS
Jeffrey Gardner

The picture on page 182 was taken on the top of the Eiffel Tower in Paris—I had tagged along with my mother while she went to a psychology conference. I remember being particularly struck by all of the statues of the revolutionary and military heroes—grim looks, hands in coats, etc. More than anything, I wanted to be like them: stoic, serious, bearing the weight of nations and kingdoms on my shoulders. I also spent a fair amount of time making weird faces, pretending I was a gargoyle—but that's neither here nor there.

I think I have a tendency to look back at pictures of myself when younger and think: How serious I was! How absolutely convinced that I was mature! Isn't it good that I've relaxed now? Or at least, now my seriousness is appropriate for my age and dignity. I think I'm always wrong—I'd probably give the same advice to this version of me that I'd like to give to my college self, and my high school persona, and looking back at my time now in five years, et al.: Loosen up! Relax! If you're wrong, it'll probably be okay!

I guess I still haven't entirely taken that in, but I like to think I'm getting closer.

I STAYED IN MY OWN WORLD
Patrick Rowland

As a skinny twelve-year-old, Kid from Kid 'n' Play influenced my hairstyle. While most of my peers were quoting NWA, I was quoting *Pee-Wee's Playhouse*, and I had a very good Pee-Wee impression as well. I grew up on Chicago's tough Westside, where I saw drugs being dealt, heard gunshots weekly, and gangs banging. Yet, I had no street smarts, because I only wanted to see the good in the world.

Being cool was the thing, and I was never cool. I still played with my GI Joes and stuffed animals. I would conduct tournaments, make brackets, and play UNO with myself, using the names of people in my class to fill out the rest of the brackets. My mother said she could never punish me by taking away toys because I would play with pens and strings on the floor. I kept to myself a lot—it was the introvert in me—but I still wanted to be accepted by the "cool" kids, so I would do things I thought would get me in good with them. Only problem is the things I thought were cool (i.e., Pee-Wee Herman, Saturday morning cartoons, and toys) were not cool to *them*. Everyone was growing up except me. They were getting ready for high school and dating and being difficult teenagers. I didn't want to grow up; I was a Toys "R" Us kid.

I loved the fun of being a kid—the wonderment and joy. I didn't want to be serious, and I didn't want to know about the ugliness of the world, so I stayed in my world. It made me feel like an outcast, though; I just couldn't relate. I would write short stories like "Nightmare on Sesame Street" and "Gary the Masturbating Goat" (that one helped me get through puberty). I always felt different, like I was from another world and I was sent down to observe how "normal" people acted. I was about to start high school, and I had to quit being a child and start being an adult if I wanted to be taken seriously and deemed "cool."

If I could talk to younger me, I would say: your imagination is what makes you unique, and being unique IS A GOOD THING. It's that imagination that will lead you to improv, and it will lead you to a community where your uniqueness is celebrated and where you can make believe all you want to.

Being different is the new cool!

WHAT ARE YOU GOING TO DO ABOUT IT, RAT BOY?

Ryan Nallen

In grade school, I was as low-status in the social realm as a kid could get. Super skinny, I had absolutely no confidence in myself. I just wanted to be liked, and I wanted to be one of the cool kids. I shouldn't have cared about that at all. But, at some point, doesn't everyone just want to be liked?

Despite being made fun of on a regular basis, I followed the cool kids around and joined them in everything they did, from joining the football team to getting in trouble. The penance I had to pay to hang out with the cool kids or to be included was their name-calling. The kids started calling me a rat. Not a rat in the sense that I told on someone or I was an informant for the mob. Instead, a rat because they thought I literally looked like one—I was short with big ears and crooked teeth. Granted, I also had a long tail and claws, *but* it was still mean.

At first, the name-calling was strictly RAT. Then, as they became clever and cleverer (mean and meaner), more nicknames were added to the list. Names like rat boy, rat fink, rat shit, and finally Master Splinter. They started saying things like "Oh, go eat some cheese" and "No rats allowed." When physical altercations presented themselves, I would hear, "What are you going to do about it, rat boy?" I would come home from school and cry my eyes out. I hated myself when I looked in the mirror.

That question—*What was I going to do about it?*—would stay with me for the rest of my life. At first, it terrified me, because it made me feel powerless and weak. It was a feeling I never wanted to feel again.

The summer before high school, I decided to make a change or *do something about it*. Cue a *Rocky*-esque montage movie sequence. While standing in front of the mirror doing barbell curls with weights that used to belong to my uncles, I'd listen to an AC/DC cassette tape on a boom box radio. Tears in my eyes. *What are you going to do about it, rat boy?* on a loop in my head.

On the football team, I was the small guy who never saw the field. Think *Rudy*. When I got to high school, one of the football coaches told me to wrestle because I would wrestle against other guys my size. *I'll kill those guys,* I thought. I weighed ninety-two pounds, but had been going against bigger guys my whole life. *These little guys don't stand a chance.* I had finally found something in which the only person responsible for my success (or failure) was me.

Every time the whistle blew, I would think: *What are you going to do about it, rat boy?*

Determination. Confidence. Perseverance.

Flash-forward through four years of high school and a wrestling record of 117 wins and 11 losses. My success didn't come from trying to prove anyone wrong; I had stopped caring about what others thought. I stopped hanging out with the so-called "cool kids" and focused on improving myself. Wrestling taught me that no matter what anyone says, anything is possible. Say it with me: ANYTHING IS POSSIBLE. It's a mind-set that I've kept with me since.

Before I left to go to college, I stood in front of the record board at my school and looked at my name and picture. I thought about how far I'd come and, more importantly, how far I was going to go no matter what career choice I made in life. I knew right then and there that I was in control of my life, and that I could be successful because I, no one else, decided it.

Absolute confidence, I thought. *That's what I'm going to do about it.*

DENYING THE LOSS OF MY MOM

Alan Linic

This picture is not of me, however much we may look alike.
But it is a part of me.

M y mother started getting really sick in the summer between my freshman and sophomore years of college. She had been manhandling chemotherapy and radiation for years, but when cancer finally caught up to her jet-propelled willpower, it stripped her of that strength in less than a week. When her lung collapsed for the first time, I drove her to the hospital at 3 a.m. to nod off in a plastic ER chair while doctors drained fluid from her chest cavity.

She spent the next month in and out of the hospital, and soon it was time to decide whether I would take time off from school to be with her or return to keep up my graduation track. Everyone insisted that my mom would want me to go back to school. When my mom was lucid enough to talk to me about it, that's exactly what she said.

I spent the first four weeks of college in silent denial while my mom was dying. I distanced myself from what was happening in my house. Not one of my friends at school even knew she was ill.

She died on September 22, 2008, which began a year and a half of numbness in my life. I became bitter and destructive in my personal relationships, drank my way through evenings and weekends, and nearly abandoned classes and extracurricular activities. I felt so incapable of connecting to anything that I turned into the polar opposite of the goofy kid my mother worked so hard to raise and protect. If she had seen me, I have no doubt she would have been heartbroken.

This awkward phase in my life had nothing to do with the way I was dressed, the activities I enjoyed, or my social skills (even though I am a fashion-less dork who functions socially by viewing other humans as logic puzzles). Those things I accepted, and those things were nurtured by my mom 100 percent. My awkward phase came from denying the loss of my mom. My awkward phase came from denying the person who made it okay to be the fun and quirky kind of awkward that I was used to being. It took me a long, long time to let my mom's spirit back into my life.

I'm never letting her or any part of myself go again.

THE START OF MY REAL LIFE
Robert Bacon

The giant glasses, horrible haircut, dead fish, and overall fatness of this photo should scream "awkward phase." The truth is, this isn't the start of my awkward phase, but the end of it. This photo was taken when I was twelve years old, and it was my first summer in the full custody of my father. Before this, I was awarded to the care of my mother after my parents separated when I was just five.

For the next seven years of my life living with my mother, I was raised in an environment of poverty, drugs, alcoholism, violence, and abuse. I didn't have many friends because we were never able to pay rent long enough to stay in one apartment so we constantly moved. Not that many kids wanted to be friends with me, anyway. I was subjected to harassment about my weight, dirty clothes, broken glasses, and always being the new kid. Things got even worse when I had to live in a long bed camper with my mother and stepfather.

When I was twelve, my father found out what was really going on and immediately gained custody of me. This photo was taken during a fishing trip to Canada that I took with my dad, uncle, and three cousins. My cousin, Steven, and I were always really close, but these fishing trips brought us closer together and made him feel like a brother to me. These are great memories and were the start of something normal for me. My dad and I lived in an actual house. I made real friends at school, and I had an extremely loving family of aunts, uncles, cousins, and grandparents. Steven was in an accident just a few years ago and passed away. I still miss him a lot and photos from these fishing trips will always remind me of him and how much fun we had together. So it might just be an extremely awkward photo of me, but it brings out so many feelings. For me, it wasn't just the end of my awkward phase, but the start of my real life.

OVERHEARD
Marianne Meyer

This is my second-grade picture. I overheard my mom talking on the phone saying that my sisters had taken very nice pictures, and *Marianne's was not such a great picture* . . . but she thought she had better order the portrait package. My exact thought at that time was: I told her I wanted the pink cat-eye glasses! (As if they would have fixed this disaster!)

To top it off, this is the first in a long series of bad haircuts by a woman named Mrs. Jinx (seriously). This little gem was not a hot commodity on the picture-trading circuit that year, mainly because I conveniently forgot to bring them to school.

My parents raised daughters who grew up to be strong, independent women. No matter how awful the glasses, the braces, the acne, the bad haircuts, we knew we were loved.

I have always felt a flow of support from them—even on picture day.

A LISP AND A SURPRISE
Shantira Jackson

I chose this photo because I remember being really excited about my look. My hair was slicked back and I had a tiny black comb in my back pocket to make sure it stayed just so. I'd been at that school for a little over a year and a half and I still wasn't cool, but I also wasn't crying regularly so I consider the time surrounding that picture day to be successful. Now, in hindsight, I'd say a lot of people dropped the ball here, but I digress.

The next day, I left the only friends I'd ever known and was sent off to my new school. On the second day of fourth grade, I showed up at W. T. Moore Elementary, where I fortunately had a class, and a teacher, but NO FRIENDS. I spent the whole day crying in front of my new classmates. Let's just say it was hard to bounce back from that.

Though I eventually stopped crying at school, I still struggled in the friend department. And it would continue until late into my teens.

I was an excitable kid, and I thought I was pretty likeable. I was just kind of waiting for everyone else to join the excitement and invite me over to their houses so we could start the best-friending. Yeah, I had giant grown-up glasses, but that wasn't my fault. It wasn't until the late nineties that people actually made kid glasses that weren't just grown-up glasses with cut-down ear thingies. And, yeah, I had a horrible lisp. My name is Shantira Jackson, and it sounded more like my name is "Thantira Jacthon." But eight-year-old me was nice, and good at basketball, and I had a massive crush on the Green Power Ranger Tommy. Who wouldn't want to befriend that?

Now, I'm gonna be real with you, I was never regularly bullied or tortured. Name-calling was sporadic and usually took place at summer camps. I was just a kid who never found a solid group of friends for the majority of my adolescence. I was lonely at school—a place filled with people whom I happened to spend eight to ten hours a day with. In an attempt to gain some solidarity, I became the class clown. Before I knew the meaning of either, I became well versed in self-deprecation and sarcasm. They seemed to work well together.

All those years of waiting to be invited to parties and wanting so badly for boys to hold my hand set me up for a life filled with love and laughter and kindness. You see, the loneliness bred confidence. As far as personality goes, not much has changed in the past fifteen years. I'm still pretty excitable, I cry regularly, and I have a PhD in self-deprecation. But I know how hard it is to want people to like you, so when I want to be friends with someone, I tell them why I think they're just great. Sometimes, I'm so overwhelmed with love for people I just hug and hug and hug and then hold hands for just a little while. Hopefully, I'm not too abrasive, but you just never know if people have been uprooted only to sit in a class of strangers.

We'll hug soon. Third-grade Thantira would love it.

PS: Shout out to all the speech therapists out there. I'm a comedian/performer now, and I wouldn't even have the confidence to say my name without your years of patience. I am forever grateful.

YOU ARE GOING TO FINALLY BREATHE

Jane Hammer

H i, baby girl. You're going through a lot right now. Your sister is taking her first photography class, and she's slated you to be her model. You like hearing the word *model* and your name in the same sentence. It means you're beautiful, although you hardly fucking believe it. But you've done your best. You've pulled your short, weird haircut up into some sort of half ponytail, you've painted your nails, and you've put on your best hemp choker. You really don't know what you think art is yet, but you're pretty sure holding a grape and looking at it like you've never seen anything like it before kind of qualifies.

You're twelve. What you don't know is absolutely no one has any idea who they are when they're twelve, and the really shitty thing about that is that it just gets worse before it gets better. You're headed toward high school, and you'll have even less of an idea how you fit in there. You have surgeries and wheelchairs ahead of you. You will be really different on the outside when that is the absolute last thing you want. You want to blend in. You want people to think you're pretty. You want people to think you're smart. You want people to think you're thin. You want people to think you're a goddamn model.

Here's the thing: you will be convinced that none of these things are true about you, but I promise you they are. You won't believe anyone who says that they are and that's okay. I think you really needed to hate yourself a little bit to be able to appreciate yourself in the future and, during that time period, you will make some of the best friends of your life.

You will meet people who will make you laugh your head off and love you even when you're confined to two wheels.

You will meet a group of girls who will never let you miss a party and will stuff your wheelchair in the back of their cars and make sure that you have enough Natty Light when you get there.

You will meet girls who will visit you in the hospital and watch you cry when you're in pain and just love you. They support you through everything, even to this day. When high school is over, you're going to be so happy. You're going to run away and find confidence. It's just going to fall into your lap in a way that you never expected.

You're going to stop focusing on the things you don't have (most of the time) and focus on all the wonderful things you do have.

You're going to realize that you want to be happy and know that you have control over that. You're going to find the most perfect friends you could ever imagine. You are going to find people who will be your lifeline. You're going to cut out the basic bitches in your life and find your rid-or-die bitches. You are going to finally breathe out the words "I'm gay," because you can't hold it in anymore. Know that anyone who loves you doesn't give a shit and probably already knew, anyway.

You are finally going to understand what it means to actually have no money. You are finally going to understand what it means that your parents have money, but you don't. You are going to understand that you don't get free reign of their bank account. You are going to eat a load of ramen because you're an "artist," and you spent all your money on shots for the entire bar last night in a blackout of generosity you can't afford. To supplement your income, you're going to work at a restaurant and when that one woman calls you a bitch, you're going to spit in her food and not feel an ounce of regret about it to this day.

You're going to have days where you look at this picture and laugh because you didn't know anything. You're also going to have days where you look at a selfie you posted on Instagram and laugh because you still don't know anything.

But I promise you, you will be happy and proud of everything that you've been through, and you will never be ashamed of who you are, ever again.

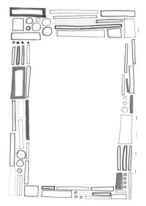

YOUR STORY HERE

Step 1: Find a picture of you in the midst of . . . let's call it, well, you know, an AWKWARD PHASE.

Step 2: Breathe.

Step 3: Write your young self a note.

Step 4: Read it aloud.

Step 5: Do a dance—shoulder-shimmy if you're in a crowd (or at work).

We love that you've spent this time with us. We hope we made you smile, because we love to see you smile. Please remember, you can always sit with us.

Peace, Love & Braces,
The Awkward Kidz

Contributor Bios

Brooke Allen is a playwright and nonfiction storyteller in Chicago. Her plays have been produced throughout the United States and London. She is a regular performer with Chicago's hit Live Lit shows, including "You're Being Ridiculous," "The Paper Machete," and "Mortified." She still hates dancing and loves her cat, Fig.

Robert Bacon graduated from the University of Wisconsin Oshkosh with a degree in speech communication and was in the United States Marine Corps Reserves. He is now an actor and comedian who lives in Chicago with his cat Mayor McCheese.

Danny Bergman lives with his wife, children, dogs, cats, and turtle near Wichita, Kansas. He is a professor of science education and blogs at www.teachlikeasuperheroblog.com. When he's not writing, teaching, or shepherding his kids/pets, Danny tweets @danieljayberg. Recently, Danny achieved professional skateboarder status—on the Nintendo Wii Fit.

Kelly Bird is a marketing enthusiast living in Colorado. She remains one of the few people in the state who is terrified of skiing. She adores dogs, blushes at swear words, and her apartment has numerous novels strewn about in various stages of being read. Her sister is still blond and adorable.

Ryann Bird feels empathy for inanimate objects, she separates her M&Ms by color before eating, and she wears a parka at least four months of the year. She is a client relations specialist who actually enjoys being on the phone all day. She is working on stamps for her passport and a dog for her lap.

Laura Bloechl is an actress and comedian in Chicago. She hasn't had bangs since 1996. @LauraBlaykul

Raised in Montana, **Erin Claxton** decided the sky was too big and hit the road. She has spent the past four years in Chicago improvising, running, cheering for sports, eating, and drinking. She has become a self-proclaimed designer and chef thanks to HGTV and Food Network. Maybe she'll cook you something.

Spensaur Cooper is one half of the indie dance band The Super Cutes. You can find him on Tumblr at talesfromthetown.tumblr.com.

Gaby Dunn is a writer, journalist, comedian, and YouTuber living in Los Angeles. She is not fun.

Bente Engelstoft is an actor, writer, and comedian. She has been performing in Chicago for the last seven years on the stages of Second City, iO Chicago, and The Annoyance Theatre. When she's not performing, Bente spends her time teaching people how to pronounce her name. It's like "Brenda" without the R.

Ashley England is a proud Buffalo, New York, native and Chicago comedian. She is grateful to her family and friends for encouraging her in all things life, love, and the pursuit of happiness; to her awkward phase for making her who she is today; and to Tyler and Claire. www.ashengland.com

Cathie English grew up in the gloriously hip '70s in Silver Creek, Nebraska, the fifth child in a family of twelve, which necessitated honing her very loud and outspoken voice. She is mother to two of the most sarcastic children ever raised and grandma to the cutest grandchildren in the world.

Suzy Exposito is a staff illustrator at *Rookie*. Nowadays, she keeps archives of her middle/high school diaries at 8thgrademallgoth. tumblr.com.

Native Texan, Harvard graduate, and accidental YouTube technologist, **Kathleen Fitzgerald** is an alumna of The Second City's sketch-writing program, iO, and *Mortified*'s featured storyteller series. She currently lives, writes, and edits video shorts in the arctic tundra of Chicago. Follow her @kafitz.

Jeffrey Gardner is the executive producer of *Our Fair City* (www.our-faircity.com), an audiodrama about (among other things) how awkward life will be after the apocalypse.

A Chicagoan by way of Texas, **Kelley Greene** spends her days troubleshooting computers for a well-known Internet company. By night, she furiously writes novels. The remainder of her time is spent obsessing over how adorable her dog is and maintaining her numerous collections so she doesn't end up on *Hoarders*.

Michael Greenwald is currently a social worker in Chicago, specializing in mental health. His form of self-care is improvising and writing. His least favorite game is Truth or Dare.

Sara Grossman is a Floridian New Yorker living in Denver. When she isn't busy (still) obsessing over JTT and wishing her mom hadn't thrown her shirt away, she works as a social media specialist and puts her MFA to good use doing it! Want more awkward? Follow her on Twitter: @sosarasaid.

Caroline Harrington is thirty-five years old (going on fifteen) and hails from exciting Wallingford, Connecticut (one of the towns that inspired *Gilmore Girls*). She has spent over a decade in Los Angeles, where she resides with her boyfriend and two cats. She strives to be equal parts awesome and awkward on a daily basis and is proud to have inspired the "Hobo Debbie Gibson" trend that seems to be so popular with kids these days.

Jane Blackburn Hammer is a sometimes comedian who lives and works in Chicago. Although she lives in Chicago, please do not get it twisted, she is from Cambridge, Massachusetts, and will be an East Coast b*tch for life. You can follow her on Twitter for her quarterly tweets at @blackburnhammer and basically find her on all social media under the same name.

Erin Hickey eventually grew up and has had as many as eight successful auditions since the age of seven. When she's not on stage or g-chatting her friends all day at work, she attempts to get fit by getting off the couch to bake more muffins. You can find her cook-book in stores probably never because that would require a lot of work and she's fairly lazy.

Michael Hinder currently tutors math to college students and loves it. Being awkward is and forever will be a regular part in my life and that's okay! Thanks for reading this book and celebrating being awkward!

Shantira Jackson moved to Chicago in 2009 to pursue a career in comedy. She is an inaugural Bob Curry Fellow who has trained and performs at The Second City, iO Chicago, The Annoyance Theatre, and ComedySportz. She is thankful for all of the awkward years that led to this point.

Erin Lann is a comedian and landlord in Chicago. She enjoys hiding mail from tenants she doesn't particularly like. When she's not writing or performing, she loves traversing the globe with her best friend/emergency contact. She wants to see a sunrise on every continent, and a sunset over every ocean.

Lyndsay Legel is an Iowa farm girl who lives in Oak Park, Illinois, with her cutie-tootie husband Phil. She is a teacher, a writer, and a burgeoning ukulele player. While the peak of her Reba McEntire obsession dates back many years, she still hopes to one day meet the red-haired wonder.

Alan Linic is a member of The Second City Tour Co. He lives with his wife Claire in Chicago and they both treat their dog Oboe like a son.

Rebecca Loeser is a stand-up comic. She acts in Video Palace films, and co-founded alt-comedy group All of Our Feelings at Once, as well as theater company Buzz22. Because she occasionally appeared on *Sesame Street* as a child, Rebecca has danced with Savion Glover, which remains the sexiest thing about her.

Dawn Luebbe is a Los Angeles–based writer and actor. Her book of comedic essays and preteen diary entries, *My 1992 Diary*, was published by Abrams in 2015. She is a performer and producer with Upright Citizens Brigade Digital. She has been seen on CollegeHumor, NickMom, UCB Comedy, and the web series *High Maintenance*.

Mitchell Lyon has spent his entire life making tiny films for fun and profit. He studied video production at The Art Institute of Colorado and currently owns and operates two companies, Shift Worship and Fortunate Pictures. Originally from Lincoln, Nebraska, Mitchell now lives in Chicago with his wife and son and about a gazillion other people.

Niki Madison enjoys dancing to live music, fashion and pop culture of the 1980s and 1990s, and cats. She holds a BA and an MS in communication and a BA in graphic design. She is a media researcher and a big, black Chicago woman doing her thing . . . like Oprah was . . . but she's broke.

Marie Maloney is an actor/improviser, writer, and all-around good-time gal who works at various theaters around Chicago. If you'd like to see her perform or verify if she still wears Twirl Test–approved dresses, feel free to visit her website at http://mariemaloney.com to see where she's playing next!

Eli Mandel is a comedian living in Chicago. If you're around town, you can see him perform at the iO and CIC theaters. If you're out of town, check out the "Improvised Star Trek" podcast, where he plays Acting Doctor Rip Stipley. Eli hails from O'Neals, California.

Irene Marquette is an actor, director, and creator based in Chicago who works every day to make her weird younger self proud. She curates and hosts "The Curio Show"@irenechicago; www.irenemarquette.com

Stephen McDonald currently produces documentaries for Vice Media and spends his weekends building concrete lamps. His nights usually consist of spending far too much time on the Internet mentally debating which is cuter: baby elephants or baby hippos. The world may never know but he will not stop digging for the truth.

David Meyer is a genetic engineer who lives with his wife Marianne, dog Penny Lane, and sometimes Congo the Cat in Indianapolis. He is the biggest science fiction nerd in any room and loves being a grandfather.

A young **Marianne Meyer** read a children's book on Clara Barton and dreamed about growing up to be a registered nurse. She is now living that dream in Indianapolis and absolutely loves being a new grandma.

Sylvia Miller is from Walnut Grove, a small town in southwest Missouri. She now lives in Chicago after obtaining her master of divinity degree from McCormick Theological Seminary. Currently, she works as the children and youth director at a church in the suburbs of Chicago and loves spending her free time with her boyfriend watching sci-fi and drinking local beers.

Ryan Nallen is an actor, writer, and improviser in Chicago. He is an improv/sketch graduate of iO, The Second City Conservatory, and The Annoyance Theatre, as well as a contributing writer for Elite Daily, Thought Catalog, and The Second City Network.

Shannon Noll is a comedian living in Chicago. When not performing, she can be seen riding her bike and cheating on veganism with copious amounts of cheese.

Wes Perry was recently named one of *Paper Magazine*'s 10 Comedians You Need to Know. Wes uses his background in improvisation and sketch comedy to create original solo pieces that blend storytelling and music in a way that's unique, honest, and absurd. He is the host of the monthly variety show *Making Out with Wes Perry and Friends*. *Making Out* originally ran at the Upstairs Gallery, where it broke box office and attendance records. *Making Out* is currently running every third Wednesday of the month at Flat Iron Comedy. Wes can also be seen performing with The Awkward Phase and Holy Fuck Comedy

Hour at The Annoyance Theatre, The Curio Show at The Mission Theater, or Second Date at Wangs. yeshairy on Tumblr and Instagram.

Patrick Rowland was born and raised in Chicago, where he still resides. Patrick performs and teaches improv at the world-famous iO Theater. When he is not making people laugh he enjoys spending his free time watching TV and drinking wine with his girlfriend Sylvia. Learn more about Patrick at www.patrickrowland.com. Follow your dreams!

Alison Sinclair, the fiery freckle-faced corn-fed husker fan born and raised. She is a true social worker at heart, striving to improve children's lives daily. She has a sparky personality, definitely is not a writer, and isn't into tweeting!

Kenneth Soltis was born and raised in New Orleans. He is currently an MFA candidate in nonfiction at the University of New Orleans and an associate nonfiction editor of *Bayou*, the university's national literary magazine.

Shaun Sperling is an attorney, writer, civil rights activist, motivational speaker, and performer. A video of him performing Madonna's "Vogue" at his 1992 Bar Mitzvah went viral in August 2012, receiving over 1.1 million views. Now, Shaun is working to spread a message of authenticity, self-respect, compassion, and acceptance through speaking engagements and workshops for high schools, universities, and corporations.

Jessica Stopak is a corn-bred Nebraskan currently residing in Chicago as a stagehand for the Goodman Theatre. She is a Disney and Muppets enthusiast. She has made being a bridesmaid a profession with seven dresses and counting in her closet. Tom Hanks continues to be one of her many idols.

Helene Sula is a blogger at *Helene in Between*, where she tries to recount the minute details of her life, like how to find the perfect sunset spot in Santorini, Greece. When she's not blogging, she's probably Instagramming pictures of her hands and drinking Diet Coke.

Edie Talley, an award-winning journalist, is completing her MFA in creative nonfiction at the University of New Orleans, where she has served as the editor-in-chief of UNO's student newspaper, *Driftwood*, managing editor of UNO's literary journal, *Ellipsis*, and is the current associate nonfiction genre editor of UNO's literary magazine, *Bayou*.

Lucy Waters is a senior admissions officer for Columbia College Chicago and Second City Training Center Conservatory graduate. She lives in Chicago with her partner Kyle and has a hobbit-like appreciation of cheese. Lucy is thrilled and excited to be a part of *The Awkward Phase*.

Taylor Wolfe is a Chicago-based comedian. You can follow her on The Daily Tay via her Twitter (twitter.com/thedailytay) and website (http://www.thedailytay.com/).

Acknowledgments

TYLER

Claire Linic: Wow. If my Tumblr-archive-checking skills are accurate, the publication of this book will occur almost exactly three years after our first *Awkward* post in the museum break room. In that time, you've gotten married and have become a dog owner. I got a really bad sunburn in Florida and ate a Most American Thickburger in Texas. But I won't brag too much. Anyway, I want to thank you from the bottom of my heart emoji for being a FRIEND (yes, *Golden Girls* reference) but also, like, for real, you are the best awkward friend ever ever ever, and I love you.

Lauren MacLeod: You are probably the only lit agent on EARTH who could so understand and support my love for Rihanna. Also, you're one of the funniest/best people I've met through the Internet and GREAT at your job. **Annoyance Theatre in Chicago:** I love you for letting us put on Awkward Phase Live for over a year. **Rachel Fershleiser:** You're so good at Tumblr, and your support was super important to us in the blog's earliest days. **Nicole Frail:** Your editing skillz are mad on-point, and I need to thank you the most for not making fun of my utter lack of DPI knowledge.

All the awkward kids, in this book and on the Internet, you are all stars to me!!!!!!!!!

<3 Tyler

CLAIRE

Tyler Gillespie: Becoming your friend and creative partner is one of the best things to happen to me. Creating and nurturing this project together has been a great adventure and I can't believe the book is finally here. Thank you for all the celebrity gossip and for always answering my crazy texts. You are my awkward heart's soul mate. Love for life.

Lauren MacLeod: I'm sorry for treating you like my big sister, diary keeper, MVP, and lit agent all rolled into one. I don't know how to be cool around you. Your support of Tyler and me since day one has been unwavering and this would have never happened without you. **Annoyance Theatre in Chicago:** Tyler and I are so lucky to be a part of your supportive and super-weird family. Thank you for giving us a home. **Rachel Fershleiser:** Girl. Girl. Girl. I cried twice trying to write this section. I'll just simply say thank you for everything. You and the whole Tumblr crew have been so good to us. **Nicole Frail:** We got thrown into this together and I could not feel luckier. Every writer deserves to experience your magic editing touch. I hope in our Lifetime movie this is described as our first of many projects together. **Alan Linic:** You have been my partner since the minute I met you. Thank you for all the behind-the-scenes work you have done on this project. I love you. Could you do the morning dog walk tomorrow?

To all my awkwards out there. Keep shining. I see you. I support you. I love you.